Praise for E
Inner Entrepreneur

“What if achieving your dreams and leaving a loving, lasting legacy were really possible? What if there were a step-by-step process for creating your vision and making it happen?
What if you could get past the fear of starting or growing your business?
It's all possible and it can start for you by purchasing this book and implementing its strategies. David Cohen holds your hand through the uneasy parts of growing and celebrating your business.
There is no excuse not to begin realizing your dream anymore.
David's integrity and honest, “down-home” style is exactly what any business person needs to move forward. From structure to sales, motivation to marketing—this book is a resource every business person should have on their desk.”
~Barry Spilchuk, Coauthor of *A Cup of Chicken Soup for the Soul®*/The Trusted Authority in Video Coaching
www.YouCanCafe.com

“David Cohen has written THE definitive book for anyone who wants to own their own business without having it own them! He has gone through all the detailed steps of how to work through the transition of working for others to working for yourself. By following the expert advice David Cohen has compiled, you are sure to succeed beyond your dreams! If you can only buy and read ONE book before you start your venture, then choose this guide as your business bible!”

~Ellie Kay, America’s Family Financial Expert ®/Author of 14 books including *The Sixty Minute Money Workout* (Random House)

"David's book is an invaluable resource for anyone who is thinking of starting a business or has already dived in head first into the complicated terrain of self-employment. The book delivers accessible, smart, witty, advice on how to attract clients, deal with rejection and be creative with "selling" yourself and your product! A must read for all!"
~Trey Anthony, Producer, writer and actor in the award winning play and TV Show *'da Kink in My Hair*

"David is a hall of fame hugger! He has been helping people and companies through radio and consulting....and now as an author where he delivers lots of ideas for every reader in his new book!"
~Jack Mitchell, Author of *Hug Your Customers & Hug Your People* and CEO of the Mitchells Family of Stores

"*Bust Out* is more than a great book title. It's about taking your inner self and projecting it into everything you do in your business. As you swiftly evolve, your business will follow. David Cohen gets it. 'Good fortune favors the bold' is something he truly understands."
~Jim Fannin, World's #1 Coach of Champions

"With this book, it feels like David takes your BIG VISION into his capable hands, holds it for you gently, then says, "Let's make this happen. Here's how." He understands boomers, has been where you are and knows where you can go. This book is all about whole-hearted inspiration, pragmatism and a deep commitment to your success."
~Tanya Geisler, CPCC/Life and Business Coach, www.tanyageisler.com

"David Cohen offers practical and easy to understand content with clearly laid out, step by step action items to powerfully move you along your path to building a strong small business. This comprehensive book will take your abstract idea and give you all the tools you need to bring it into reality...from dealing with the legal stuff and creating your business structure, to marketing both online and offline, to mastering the sales cycle and closing deals. A must read for business owners both in the beginning and advanced stages."
~Cindy Ashton, Singer/Entertainer, Speaker, Author & Artist/Speaker Coach, www.CindyAshton.com, www.SimpleStepstoStardom.com

"David Cohen is a great coach and human being, whose intent behind everything he does is to make the world a better place. His book [Bust Out] reflects his coaching in that he balances the importance of the nuts and bolts of doing business with how to manage work/life, something of immense importance to entrepreneurs, especially start-ups, when they are wearing so many of the hats. [Bust Out] will not only give you the practical information and motivation you need to build your business, but also nuggets of wisdom that will help you bring joy and spirit to the process and beyond."
~Tiina Veer, BA RMT RYT/Founder of Yoga for Round Bodies™/Steward, Halcyon Health Wellness Centre

"David Cohen shares years of wisdom and inspiration in *Bust Out: Ignite Your Inner Entrepreneur."*
~Kelly McCormick, Author of OutSell Yourself: Go From Hello to Sold with Ethical Business and Sales Techniques!, Business Expert/Speaker/Consultant/Coach

"David Cohen has created a book that is practical, filled with ideas that had me rethinking how I do business. He is someone I respect deeply, as he runs every part of his life with such integrity. This book is filled with juiciness in every corner."
~Jennifer Hough, Creator of the *Get Out of Your Own Way* Course and CEO of The Vital You

"David's infectious inspiration is woven into the fabric of his new book. I say *infectious* because you can't help but "catch it" through the intention, tone and information relayed within the words and pages.
Following the layout of his book is like having a knowledgeable guide on a long hike. At the start of the journey you are excited and hopeful to make the trek. With a great guide, at some point on the path you are no longer focused on the effort you must make, you now are focused on the sights and vision in front of you. This is a guide book.
Through the success stories, examples and tips in this handbook David gives you the tools to map your vision and make your dream a reality."
~Michele Meiche, Broadcaster, teacher and Author of *Meditation for Everyday Living*

"David is an ideas guy. One of the best. When he facilitates or coaches our clients they always love his stories and are impressed by his quick mind and creative ideas. This book is filled with great stories and comes packed full of those same razor-sharp ideas.
~Ian Kennedy, Managing Director of Essential Communicatons, Ltd.

"David Cohen has written the essential guide to starting and staying in business. It offers simple, easy to use tools and ideas that will have you saying, "Why didn't I think of that?" Which is the greatest compliment you can give to any advisor."
~Lou Schizas, Business Analyst for Talk Radio AM 640 Toronto

"Through useful tips, cutting edge ideas and a series of engaging workshops, David Cohen helps the boomer entrepreneur to achieve true business success in BUST OUT!"
~Catrina Warner, CBC TV- News Editor

"David's book is a must read for anyone looking to "bust out" and jump into their business venture. Through his knowledge and insightful advice David gives you what's important, 'cuts to the chase', with a strong action plan, an intuitive road map, that will get you going on the right track and ignite your passion to succeed."
~Rachael McDonald, Virtual Business Assistant and Visual Artist

Bust Out!

Ignite Your Inner Entrepreneur

Boomer Edition

By David Cohen

ABC
PUBLISHING

Bust Out! Ignite Your Inner Entrepreneur

All inquiries should be addressed to:

A Better Choice Publishing
41 Temperance Street, P.O. Box 2,
Clarington, ON L1C 3A0
Phone: 888-700-8414
Email: contact@abcpublishing.org

First Edition

ISBN: 978-0-9866789-6-7

WARNING-DISCLAIMER

This book is intended to provide information about starting a small business. It is also meant to inspire and encourage you to overcome fear and take the steps necessary to get started. It is sold with the understanding that the publisher and the author is not engaged in providing business counseling.

We have tried to make this book as complete as possible; however there may be mistakes, both typographical and in content.

The purpose of this book is to educate, motivate and entertain. The authors and A Better Choice Publishing shall have neither liability nor responsibility to any person or entity with respect to any loss or damage caused, or alleged to have been caused, directly or indirectly, by the use of the information contained in this book or from any website mentioned in the book.

If you do not wish to be bound by the above, you may return this book to the publisher for a full refund.

Contents

AFTERWORD

Foreword

By Rick Spence

I was once asked to offer my best advice for small business owners—in three words.

Saying something meaningful in three words is quite a challenge. But you learn quickly that three words can pack a lot of punch—if they're the right words. "Rejoice, we conquer." "I shall return." "Seize the day." "I love you."

Under pressure, I offered the advice: "Make the call."

After more than 20 years of working with entrepreneurs, as a writer, editor, consultant or director, I no longer believe in natural limits. Unimaginable success awaits business owners who deliver great products or services, target their markets, hire the right people, and create mutually profitable relationships with their customers, employees and suppliers. Not everyone will succeed—just as not every writer will pen a best-seller, and not every baseball player will bat .300. But I am convinced that the *possibility* to survive and thrive is greater than ever.

Still, you have to make the call. The one you've been putting off, because it's just so important to your business. It's probably a call to a key customer or distributor, but it could also be a call to a potential partner, the bank, or a supplier you need to wangle a deal out of. In my career, the biggest obstacle business owner's face is their reluctance to make these calls. They may be afraid of being rejected, or they may feel their business isn't ready. What they don't realize is that this call *is* the business. Business is about *people* making *connections* —not about ideas locked up in your head, products sitting in a warehouse or production equipment waiting to be unpacked. For all the reasons I'm about to go into, success is abundant in this brave new economy—but it accrues only to those who recognize that courage and passion are your own best source of competitive advantage.

"Making the call" separates the doers from the dreamers and heaven knows the reward is waiting.

A number of different factors and trends have combined to make running your business not just rewarding, but potentially life changing. Here are just a few of those factors that have turned the economics of business upside down by putting the tools of success into the hands of every capable individual:

New communications technologies—from the cell phone to Google—let us reach more people, master more market data, and become prominent players in our industries faster and more easily than ever before.

More flexible and affordable supply chains let us contract out the manufacturing of products or development of services, freeing entrepreneurs to focus on what they do best: seeing opportunities and bringing buyers and sellers together.

International logistics partners (think UPS, Fedex, etc.) help us connect with best-of-breed producers anywhere in the world, and ship goods to market faster and more accurately than ever before.

Burgeoning new marketing channels, from Facebook to YouTube, enable highly focused entrepreneurs to reach niche markets globally, for a fraction of the cost of print advertising that was the standard a decade ago.

Growing armies of freelance experts—from product designers and engineers to copywriters, accountants and sales coaches—are available on demand to fill the gaps in your business team and ensure your team exudes professionalism—in product quality, communications, and internal systems and standards.

Best of all, big businesses, government agencies and other five-star prospects now recognize that great ideas and business breakthroughs are not confined to corporate laboratories or Wall Street conglomerates. Big organizations are more willing than ever to work with (or buy from) high-quality, focused companies, big or small, that create value through unique products and services.

If there's been a better time to be in business, I can't imagine when it was.

A few years ago, I interviewed Seth Godin, the popular U.S. author and marketing guru who has pioneered thinking around Internet-era business and marketing. He believes the changes in IT alone (the Net, email, social media, outsourcing) constitute a new industrial revolution. In our conversation, I took that argument and extended it, suggesting to him that this is one economic upheaval tailor-made for knowledgeable, focused *individuals* who are committed to conducting ambitious, meaningful ventures of their own. Godin agreed, saying he thinks this is the best time *in history* to start a business of your own. He said: "If someone had sat down 15 years ago and said, 'How can we create an atmosphere that's conducive to startups?', what they would have come up with is what we have today."

"What wins now," said Godin, "is speed, transparency, authenticity and passion. And all these things come from people, not faceless corporations."

What wins now are people and their commitment to personal and business excellence.

In the "old days" (before the PC, cell phones, the Net and global for-hire logistics systems), what won was capital. Factories, expensive production equipment, offices filled with bureaucrats and stenographers. The individual was a cog in the machine.

Now we are living in an age where, as Einstein noted decades ago, "imagination is more important than knowledge." Anything you can conceive, any product or service, you can find someone to build or provide. But only you—who had the imagination to think of it, and the creativity to link it to a specific market, customer type or user group—can turn the product or service into a healthy, sustainable business. Big businesses will always have a role, doing the things that massive capital is good at—producing and selling standardized products in predictable formats across an entire country or around the world (think of organizations such as McDonald's, Tim Hortons, Wal-Mart, Disney and Merck). But increasingly, small businesses and entrepreneurs top off these markets with offerings that provide higher quality, better service, or lower prices (think of the lightning-like market penetration of Starbucks, Dollarama, or Five Guys Burgers). Your product knowledge and market insight, together, can shake up your industry.

In my years of editing and writing for PROFIT Magazine and the National Post, I have met thousands of entrepreneurs who have succeeded beyond their wildest dreams—simply by offering a better-articulated value proposition to a market that they felt needed something better. In these times of seeming endless economic stagnation, it's essential that people understand that success is still possible—in fact, it's happening all around us. But success doesn't happen to just anybody. Success favors capable, prepared and disciplined visionaries the way dogs run to the nearest telephone pole. Success cannot be predicted—but it will come from predictable components:

- a personal passion for hard work, and a hunger to win;
- deep market knowledge, coupled with an eagerness to keep learning;
- a commitment to innovation and product quality;
- the ability to remain institutionally flexible, and turn on the proverbial dime;
- rock-solid integrity and commitment to ethical behavior (*especially* when no one is looking), and to crafting win-win deals with every customer, supplier or business partner;
- vivid communication skills that encourage people not just to trust you, but to want to *help* you carry out your market mission.

We probably all know a few people who have succeeded despite lacking one or more of those characteristics. But compromising on any one of these entrepreneurial traits could seriously set back your business or reduce the chances of achieving lasting success. Anybody can make one sale—but it's the repeat sale to the same customer that builds sustainable businesses.

It's unfortunate that more people don't realize how deeply the vein of opportunity runs through society today. In my experience, the people most responsible for conveying information, values, attitudes to society at large—teachers, media, governments—don't really understand how the economy has changed, so the message isn't getting out. As a result, our children grow up thinking they are in a land of endless recession rather than infinite opportunity. Fortunately, there are a few role models—the Bill Gates, Steve Jobs and Mark Zuckerbergs of this world—whose success cuts through the collective fog and demonstrates that there is another way to work, to achieve personal success and, oftentimes, great personal satisfaction.

Canada has fewer of these A-list role models. Robert Herjavec, Arlene Dickinson and the other entrepreneurs on Dragons' Den have become household names, and many Canadians still revere the team of Mike Lazaridis and Jim Balsillie, who built a superstar business at Research in Motion before taking their eye off the ball in recent years.

Fortunately, in Canada we also have people like David Cohen, who employ their personal passions and vision to building an entrepreneurship culture in other ways. David is committed to aiding, abetting, informing and celebrating Canadian entrepreneurs, in his work, his volunteer activities, and his radio show. He has devoted his career to building a more entrepreneurial culture, and to strengthening those entrepreneurs for the tests that lie ahead. In this book, he lays out today's business challenges and some of the best tactics, strategies and solutions he has encountered. Like many business coaches, economic-development consultants, enlightened entrepreneurship profs and even a few government fieldworkers, David is an unsung hero of the entrepreneurial revolution, helping to "build capacity" among ordinary Canadians in a way that will contribute to innovation, job creation and business growth across the country.

With this book, David brings together the insights he's gained and lessons learned from working with entrepreneurs in every field. As you will see, his passion and energy infuse the entire book, and his commitment to your success permeates every page. Best of all, he draws from so many diverse experiences and examples that you will realize that there is not just one way to succeed. Running your own business is an art form that's as much about your talent and commitment as it is about the wants and needs of your target market. Every entrepreneur will approach an opportunity differently (consider the varying approaches of Bill Gates and Steve Jobs). Your endeavours will have the greatest chance of success if you combine topnotch business talent (and don't worry—if you don't have it you can hire it) with your personal approach to your market and your own exuberant, confident personality. When all that "busts out" businesses thrive and communities grow. And you will be the hero you were meant to be.

Read this book. Make the call. Be the change.

Acknowledgements

I thank everyone I met along the way on my life journey. Early in my career people like Bob Templeton, Bob Bennett, Don Peter, Uncle Jerry and Victor Arluk they helped me to get started in my career. There is a key woman who believed in me through a time that was rougher than usual...Eileen Mac Isaac...I owe you a big thank you...Eileen taught me, that if there is no need, there is no business...basic truth, yes, but still meaningful. Kelly McCormick too, she showed me it was possible to succeed in a totally new career...and still is my angel to this day, 12 years later!

Plus I am thankful to some key friends: Bob the accountant; my amazing work colleagues and friends, Todd, Catrina, Carol Ann, Garth, Shawn, Angela, Jennifer, Tom, Cate, Kim, Tiina, Mark D., Marshall, Tad, Dennis, Jae, Traci, Zsuzanna, Peter and Lu, Kevin, Iain, Brian for making me laugh, Mark, Barry, Bob G, Hunter, Ron and Wenda. I have some of my personal heroes too: Jack Canfield who taught me you can be successful, spiritual and classy; Jack Mitchell who teaches the importance of hugging your customers and looking well dressed at the same time; Rick Spence who graciously wrote the foreword and is a star in Canada in the writing world; and Jim Fannin, Coach of Champions, who actually called me to congratulate me on the book. Little things go a long way let me tell you!

Also people that helped me from the early stages of the book: Dani, Darri, Peter F and Peter M from LEF and Peter M from Essential, Ian, Bev, Tina, Sue, Peter and

Murray, Shelley, Graham, Jim, Silja, Daryl, Benjy, Sue (my web designer), Jeff Tidd, Jean and Susan from Alterna Savings, (my bankers and I love them) —to the final stages: the fantastic editing done by Carolyn, who held my hand and kept me on track, and to Robin and Eric from ABC Publishing. I love that they have a dream and a niche market as far as books go and I love what they stand for as a publishing business.

I want to thank Aina-Nia, Kay and Richard at Microskills for allowing me to do work I love and to teach the lessons I talk about in the book and Kim C. for helping me live my vision! I must acknowledge my coach Tanya Geisler, she rocks! I want to thank the team at Job Skills too, Catherine, Sanja and Sonja. Oh and I would be remiss if I didn't thank Landmark Education...what they teach people helps them to do big things and live big lives day in and day out around the globe!

I also have to mention two people in my life, Jordyn and Sheryl, who taught me the three hardest lessons: letting go, loving yourself and patience.

Kudos go out to the ghost readers, Jan Wristen, Allen Kohn, Huma Mehmood, Debra Fraser, Yvette Murray, Tine Sughrue, Tamara McKee, Mena Canonico, Vicki Manning, Rachael McDonald and Mashhood Ahmed.

I am grateful for my family: my fantastic older sisters, Jan and Deb and my almost-sister Arlene and brother-in-law Jerome. Jan helped me on this journey to self-discovery and personal development. I am so thankful to my family—they keep me grounded and make sure I don't get a big head and we have fun together. I must honour my late father Phillip, my late sister Ruth and brother-in-law Gerry. I am most grateful to my late mom. She recently passed away from pneumonia and had been living with Alzheimer's for close to nine years. She had no idea I would write this book, but somehow, I know she'd be proud. My mom taught me to face any challenge with grace and dignity; I miss her and love her. I come from a good family, we've had our challenges but we always manage to laugh and enjoy the good times that life has to bring too. They are a big part of my work and success and I love them.

I also thank God for instilling in me a willing spirit to help others and lead a life of peace!

Introduction

I have never written a book before but like most things in life I was not about to let that stop me. I am a big believer of what you *think about* you can *do*. There is always someone who can help or resources you can tap into. Someone has done what you want to do and can teach you how it's done.

But this book is not about me, it's about you! It's about *you* living your best life. It's about *you* doing what you dream of doing. It's about *you* taking a risk and it's about *you* really acting on an idea that you're passionate about and making it happen.

Now you're probably thinking, "Okay...I am reading this book by a guy who has never written one before and I am going to take what he has to say to heart? Come on, right? Who's trying to pull one over on me?"

So here is the deal. Put the book back down then...and walk to the history section. Yes, there you will find many true stories of those who have accomplished something in life. Some have wreaked havoc on the world and on others and some have done remarkable acts. There are lessons to be learned from these stories.

So go on...walk over to the history section of this bookstore and check out something there. Hey who knows, maybe the store clerk in the history section is cute and single...you may even strike up a riveting conversation about Socrates or Rousseau. Or, you can begin to ignite your passion and your dream. It's your choice.

Good! You've decided to stick it out in this section of the bookstore. You've decided to give *you* a chance. I honour your commitment and if I was there I would "high five" you, but I am not, so there will be no "high fiving" yet. Remember this book is about *you*. It's about *you* succeeding.

Now tell me...if you're like most of us right about now...we've had it up to here with all the uncertainty in the world. As I begin to write this I realize it's the 9th of September—another anniversary of the day the world changed forever. That horrific day has impacted how we live, think, act and who we are.

I don't know about you but that event got me into action...I quit smoking soon after, and also took off 50 pounds. My logic was that if this was it for the planet then I for one was going out on top! I know some of you would throw in the proverbial towel and start smoking and drinking if things were coming to an end, but I chose to go out the best person I could be.

Why not be your best you? And what does that mean? You have to put your personal baggage and limits behind you and make the decision to forge ahead. It's scary and exhilarating all at once!

The other impactful event in recent history was Hurricane Katrina. Didn't CNN ram those images down our throats 24/7 for days after that disaster? It too was tragic yet transformative. This time after the hurricane I didn't do anything as drastic as quit smoking, but I did buy a new Toyota Yaris...in case gas prices rose through the roof again like they did during the hurricane. Oh, you laugh...a Yaris? I say, yes...it's great on gas...low on *life transforming* though, I admit.

So fast forward to the fall of 2008 when the economic crisis hit. Again the media amped up the volume of fear and uncertainty and left us feeling all a little lousy about life. The good news though is that we're all still here. There are still over seven billion of us on the planet doing our thing. "Yeah us," I say!

I also say that it's time for change. It's time for "us" to start living the lives we dream, to create a world we want and to help others do the same.

So where does it start?

It starts with me. It starts with you. It starts now. In this book we will share ideas, tips and tools about selling, marketing, managing, growing, operating a business and getting money for your venture.

This book is called "Bust Out! Ignite Your Inner Entrepreneur—Boomer Edition". Why did I write a book specifically for boomers? Well, for one thing there are more people aged 51 than any other age in North America. Studies show there are more boomers opening up businesses due mostly to the global economic situation. Why is that? One reason is that our retirement funds are being depleted; another reason is that we want to stay vital and keep mentally and physically active; and, a third reason is that we need the extra money. But the best reason is...we still have a lot to offer the world—our knowledge, experience and skills!!

The book is made up of articles I have written over the years as newsletters/blogs. This book is also a collection of business notes, blog posts and ideas about how to be *your best you* in your venture. I have been working on them since I began my consulting business and radio show over 10 years ago. They were written to assist my clients and to help my listeners to be successful.

Some of the articles are personal reflections and I talk about my life pretty openly. I know I leave myself open to criticism and perhaps what I believe in you don't and that's okay, let's just agree to disagree but not lose respect for each other!

Since 2002 I've hosted a small business talk radio program called the "Small Business Big Ideas Show". I not only host it, but sell the advertising, line up the guests and keep the show fresh and entertaining. I hosted it on Saturdays in the beginning, but then for many seasons I hosted my radio show every Sunday. After a brief hiatus I'm happy to be back on the air every Monday night. I've learned a lot during these years and made many connections and friends and interviewed over 1600 people. I've spoken to leading authors, thinkers, politicians, small business owners, experts in their field and local economic development officers who have made a difference.

This book is also a compilation of wisdom and ideas from people that have inspired me—friends and associates that have helped me become who I am today. I hope they will also inspire you. I wish you a good time on your journey as you launch your business, or grow it, and to your success!

Along the way there will be opportunities for self-reflection as you participate in the several "workshops" that you'll find throughout the book. I recommend that you take advantage of these opportunities to "self-assess". It will help you to build a better business if you do.

One last thing—I do a ***lot*** of name-dropping in this book. That's okay; it's done *on* purpose and *with a* purpose. Over the years I have read a lot of books on the topics I cover in this book. I want you to *know* about them. I also suggest that you *read* them. After that you can *use the information* from them to build your business.

I've interviewed hundreds of *successful* people on my radio show. Many of them have written books or have their own business. Perhaps you will benefit from knowing about them and can draw on their wisdom and experience. (Maybe you will be able to use their services but you will have to be the judge of that yourself. Any business decision is up to you and you must decide whom you feel comfortable working with.) Information is power *if* it is used. I've given you lots of information in the pages that follow and I hope that you will make use of it to reach your goals and achieve your dreams.

Let's get started. It's time.

SECTION I

Section I is about getting your idea off the ground. What will it take to launch your business and build a foundation that will be sturdy enough to stand the test of time? This section will teach you how to begin.

I remember a colleague of mine once said that if you want to take a personal growth course you should just start a business instead. There is no better place to learn about yourself than having your own business.

There will be days when you're grumpy because things aren't going so well, or days when you want to give up or pull your hair out over a supplier who got your order wrong. You'll cry in frustration because your bank didn't come through on a loan. You're also going to have days of elation when everything comes together.

If you want to fast track your personal growth and get to see every aspect of yourself then start your business.

So are you ready? Let's launch!

PART 1: STARTING YOUR VENTURE

HAVE A VISION (OR A DARN COOL IDEA)

Any product, service or business, starts with a thought, an idea and a plan. For you to begin to live your dream you've got to begin with what it is you are passionate about. What is it that you love to do? What would you do for free?

For me as a kid it was radio. I grew up the only boy with three older sisters and my mom. I lost my dad when I was 10. I wasn't about to hang out with my sisters and do girl things...I was left to make up my own fun. I got lost in radio. Radio was my friend. Radio was my out. I loved the music, the announcers, the way the disc jockeys would entertain you and put a smile on your face...that was the *something* I wanted to do.

I remember playing records on a little mini "Singer" record player in the den and announcing the songs, just like they did on CFRA radio in Ottawa. I remember taking a penny and my hockey cards and doing the play-by-play of the hockey games on the kitchen floor or in my bedroom. My mom didn't mind because I actually buffed the floors with our floor polisher between periods—my own personal Zamboni!

I was Ernie Afaghanis, Pat Marsden and Johnny Esaw all rolled into one. All of these men were wonderful sportscasters in Canada, where I live. As a boy growing up in Ottawa (Canada's capital), sports were a fantastic outlet. It too was a world you could get lost in. I learned the statistics of all the players. I knew that Doug Favell, a goal tender for the Toronto Maple Leafs and Philadelphia Flyers, was born in Flin Flon, Manitoba. That was a stat worth knowing...or so I thought at the time. And that Henri Richard was born on February 29th, a leap day. Let's see, he's 15 years old right about now!

I was also Ken "The General" Grant, the morning show host on CFRA. He got families off to work and school while playing songs like *That Rainy Day Feeling* by the Fortunes, or with songs by Charlie Rich or Frankie Valli and the Four Seasons.

That was what I excelled at as a kid and as an adult my passion for radio has stayed with me. That's why I've hosted and produced my own radio show for the better part of 10 years.

In one of the several personal development workshops I have been on over the years I heard that what you did as a kid when you were eight or nine years old and what you were passionate about then might be the ticket for you to find your life work, your purpose and passion. Sure, I loved radio, but behind it was the art of communication.

My work shifted back in the late '90s from selling promotional marketing products to becoming a coach/facilitator. My work now has me working with small business start-ups. I help small business owners in a number of ways...usually I'm the idea guy and help with selling and marketing...but I am also a major league connector. I love connecting people to others to help them further themselves.

One thing I have learned about myself in recent years is that I am not afraid to ask people for things. I love asking people to be on the show as a guest—the bigger the guest the better too. I mean why not ask for help or for the things you want in life? You're worth it. You need to *ask* for the things you need. But, make sure you return the favour and someone else's kindness with kindness back. A thank you note goes a long way, by the way!

I had to do a lot of asking when I started the radio show. For example, I didn't own a car for the first eight weeks I did the show. I lived in North York and hosted the show in Oshawa on Saturday mornings when the transit system wasn't running at its peak. The distance from where I lived to Oshawa was about 60 km and it took about 45 minutes to get from my door to the station. I hosted the show at 9 a.m. sharp which meant I had to be at the station for 8:30 to prepare and talk to the technical producer.

No car, remember? Transit not an option and a taxi would cost a fortune. So what could I do? I would simply ask each guest I had on the show for a ride to the station. Everyone I had as a guest gladly agreed. In some cases they even bought me my morning coffee...sweet, huh?

So, you have to ask or good things won't happen. In exchange for being on the show and getting media exposure, I got a ride to the station!

The idea for the launch of my business and radio show 10 years ago came through me taking a "Create Your Vision" workshop with Kim Chernecki. The business idea was born out of a thought. It started as a thought that became an idea. Then it was a vision. It went from a well thought out idea onto paper and from paper into action and from action into reality.

Remember that the goal for this book is to help you in your journey into self-employment and to help you stay successful if you're in business already. We will talk about the key core areas that make up your business plan. I will talk about attitude, marketing, selling, planning, business operations and financial issues and we will look at the legal aspects of running a business too.

So what does it take to live your best life and realize your own business vision? You need to have a vision and learn how to overcome obstacles along the way.

Success begins with a big vision, a big cause and a dose of passion!

From time to time, I am reminded that any good business venture really does begin with a vision, but these days you want to add a pinch of "cause" and a dose of *passion* too.

WHAT'S YOUR VISION?

Blog Post, September 30, 2011

> I talk more about vision and its importance for a few reasons. The state of the world these days depends on us all having a vision for something better. It's also a new season and in my religious background, it's our New Year. In Judaism it's 5772. We've come a long way as a people and have been through many challenges and many triumphs...but at the heart of what we want and wish each other this time of year is a year of joy, health, abundance and happiness and peace for all mankind...an economy that *works* wouldn't hurt either...

But at the core of what you wish someone come any New Year or even a birthday is something kind, something good, something big!

That's what we need right now. We need to have a big vision to have peace, abundance, health and well-being for not only those we know, but for everyone we share this planet with as well.

In my recent radio interviews with Guy Kawasaki, who wrote the book *Enchantment*, one of the keys to delivering goods and services he mentioned is to have a great cause. In fact to deliver a feeling of "enchantment" to your customers you need to be aware of the three key pillars. Kawasaki suggests when and why enchantment is necessary and describes the three pillars of enchantment: likability, trustworthiness, and a great cause.

As a person and business owner you want to work on your likability factor. In business, people work with people they like. If you're looking for a job, potential bosses hire people they like. You want to work on what goes into being liked.

Being someone of your word is huge. Trust in any relationship is a key part. If you work on building your "reliability" factor and can be "trusted" upon to do the job, or be there for someone else when needed, or to be there in a crunch or when waters get rough…that is huge! Trust is huge…

Lastly, you need a great cause. What's your great cause? Are you just slugging it out in life for the money? Or is there a great cause to your life or business?

My challenge to you is to pick a cause that speaks to your heart. At Zappos, the incredible online shoe (and apparel) company, Tony Hsieh (Shay) has created an amazing culture and has launched a website and a vision all about creating happiness. In fact if you log onto http://www.deliveringhappiness.com/ you will learn about the philosophy at Zappos. It's about more than just selling shoes…there is a big vision…a cause…something else at stake that drives people to be great! A vision drives you to be great.

Don't believe me yet? Michael Gerber, book author (and guest on our show several times since 2003), writes this about having a vision in his latest book *E-Myth Mastery*, "A business without a vision is directionless. It lacks purpose. You cannot plan the future of your business if you do not have a vision. It is the starting point of any business growth plan."

Then he adds, "The vision is your unique dream. It is the image of what you want your business to become. It provides the pull factor. The vision gives you the big picture. It keeps you on track as you develop strategies and take steps to grow the business. It gives you the place to focus on when overwhelmed by the mass trivia that invades our business lives. The vision puts purpose into the business." (Gerber, Michael E. 2005. E-Myth Mastery. New York: Harper and Collins.)

Great companies have a vision, a cause and a purpose. I mean really at the end of the day it's got to be about something else than just slugging it out, day after day, just trying to earn a buck, right?

Great companies like Pike Place Fish Market decided to improve morale by becoming "world famous". You go to their fish market and it's a blast. The customer experience is fun! You even have to duck out of the way as the fish mongers at the store can usually be seen throwing fish down the aisle.

Mitchells Family of Stores (with five stores in the United States) owns beautiful high end, high service clothing stores and have adopted a "Hug Your Customers" philosophy. They deliver outstanding service and have become one of America's leading clothing retailers in terms of sales and service.

Harvey MacKay, author of *How to Swim with the Sharks Without Being Eaten Alive*, is all about service and getting to know customers. His vision is to know more about each customer than the IRS. Why is that you ask? Well, it's all about being extraordinary with your customers, knowing them, remembering them, being there for them and delivering an outstanding customer care experience. And by the way, Harvey MacKay runs a company that makes envelopes! Service is the *only* game he's got to win at in order to be successful.

So...create a vision. Play for something bigger than yourself, have a cause, have that big picture or ask yourself what legacy you want to leave.

Dr. Stephen Covey reminds us in his book *The 7 Habits of Highly Effective People* to think about what you want someone to say in your eulogy at your funeral. If you think about that for a moment is your life or business just going to be about doing it, slugging it out, making a buck...or are you going to have a big picture, a goal, a dream, a vision?

It's like the story about three bricklayers. When a man walks by the construction site he asks the first bricklayer, "How's it going?" The man replies, "Eh, it's going okay I guess. I am working hard, making some money and just laying some bricks." Then the man passes the second bricklayer and asks the same question. This man replies, "I'm laying bricks to feed my family." As he approaches the third bricklayer he says, "So, I guess you're just working hard laying some bricks, eh?" This man shakes his head and looks to the sky and says, "Oh no, I am not just laying bricks...I am building a cathedral."

So what are you doing in your business? Are you just laying bricks or are you building a cathedral?

THE JOURNEY BEGINS

This first chapter is about having the right mindset. You've got to get into business with a healthy mindset and a no-quit attitude. Being in business isn't going to be easy and if you're in one now you're probably agreeing with me. But it's not all bad news. On the contrary, being in your own venture is a chance to really do what you love. As someone who opts for the "entrepreneurship route" it's a fabulous way to really share your gifts and passions with the world or at least a few good clients.

Let's get a good mindset on and put some best practices in place. Let's get going!

Being in business can seem like a long, lonely journey...but does it have to be?

Here are some sure-fire success tips for you to take to your business.

Tip one: It's been about 10 years since I started my business. It came as a result of a job loss...and it started from nothing. I lost my job on April 19, 2002. I didn't have one client, few contacts and no money coming in. That's a lonely feeling...sometimes sinking. So what kept me going? As I reflect on life back then I think what kept me going was a burning desire to succeed.

I remember one day, about two months into launching my new venture and working for a private client as her coach, actually walking around Toronto on foot making a list of contacts for her. You see she wanted to market a "singles" event and I suggested she market to local Toronto Psychotherapists. The logic there was that they would promote her event to their clients who were seeking to be in a relationship. So I walked around to all the medical buildings in downtown Toronto and got names, contacts and made sure I got an accurate contact list for her. I wanted to be my word. It didn't matter how difficult the task was, I was determined to follow through on what I had promised my client that I would do.

Take the Canada Day long weekend almost 10 years ago when I got a training contract from a client. My computer "blue screened" on me on the Friday of the long weekend...I had a week of sessions to do starting on the Tuesday. I was going to be teaching a group of women entrepreneurs at Rexdale Microskills and I had to be ready; I had to be prepared and give them my best. But I lost all my material...never to be retrieved again.

I recall taking the TTC (the transit) at 7:30 a.m. on Canada Day to my sister's house to work there all day long preparing my seminars for the client. I thought to myself, "I am either insane to do this on a holiday (and the day was gorgeous out too) or I am committed to my success and my client's success." I smiled to myself as I rode the TTC and pondered which of the two I was...and I found contentment in knowing I was a bit of both...

I did a bang up job that week. The material I created from scratch was good and the women that attended that week of my marketing workshops got a lot out of it. So as I look at the lonely road of being in business **I believe it all starts with having a burning desire to succeed**. Sometimes you have to go where no one else will.

Tip two: The other aspect of starting a business is having a *no-quit* attitude even when others say you're wrong. As I started my consulting business I developed my practice through another organization. The owner of that consulting group wanted me to give up doing the radio show that I was just getting off the ground. My gut said no way!!! Why was that? Well, the reason I didn't give up on doing the radio show was because I had worked too hard to get it going. I wasn't about to walk away from something that brought so much joy...no way...even though my work with this consulting group may have depended on it. I felt in my heart of hearts that the radio show was a joy and after putting that energy and sweat equity into it I wasn't walking away that easily. So, **success tip number two is to have a *no-quit* attitude**, no matter what they say about you.

Tip three: My next success tip is to go around obstacles. If you focus on the obstacle you'll only see *it* in front of you. You want to know why you should look beyond the obstacles in your way? Well, you will remain painfully stuck if you don't. If you look beyond the obstacles you will see opportunity and options you never knew existed. Didn't Einstein once say that the definition of insanity is doing the same thing over and over, expecting a different result? My friends, you have to look at options each time you are faced with an obstacle.

As I mentioned before when I started my radio show I didn't own a car. I had just been working for a non-profit agency and the pay there wasn't enough for me to have a car. I loved the work, it was a solid job, but it didn't afford me the chance to own a car. You remember how I overcame this obstacle? I looked for other options and found that simply asking for help (by asking my guests to pick me up and take me into the show) was the perfect solution.

One way around obstacles is to play *what if?* Look at a problem and ask yourself, "What if we could change it? What would that look like?" *What if?* is a great question to ask when you're stuck. So...success tip number three is...**look at options not obstacles.**

Tip four: Leverage your contacts...this is such a key to success I can't even begin to tell you. I remember my early days in my business and I would work my own contacts first...getting them on board or asking for referrals from people I knew. I had a connection with them and they would gladly refer me. So if your business is slow right now, I challenge you to call on people you know and ask them who they think might be a good contact for you or who would love and benefit from what you do. You'd be surprised what might happen from asking those you know; you just might get some awesome leads.

If you figure that you know at least 50 people and if you asked each one of them who they know that might be a good contact for you in your business venture...you will soon find that they know at least two to three people each (on average). That means you will end up with about 100-150 warm prospects. **Success tip number four is to leverage your contacts and networks.** It's better to ask those you know than to approach someone you've never met. It's easier on your psyche when you make that first call.

Tip five: That brings me to my next success tip, *believe*. Yes, it sounds kind of hokey, doesn't it? You're probably thinking that I'm talking about God here, right? Yup...I am. When I was cold calling potential advertisers for the show 10 years ago I made 130 phone calls. One hundred and twenty-five people said no to me. If I didn't believe in myself and in God I would have surely stopped. Something kept me going...desire, hunger, belief. Belief is the trump card my friends...it really is. If you aren't "walking the talk" you're going to fall over when the waves of negativity come at you. **Believe. Believe. Believe.**

Still don't *believe* me? When I was doing the cold calling I mentioned above I remember getting rejected by a prospect...and they were rather rude in doing so too. I looked up to the heavens and yelled at God. I had a temper tantrum right in my own home office. I said to God, "Look buddy, I need your help here...if you want me to live my dreams and do good work I need some clients and now!" (I wasn't too demanding, was I?)

The next client I called on was the Dunbarton Fairport United Church and I spoke to Reverend Glenn Brown. Why a church you ask? Reverend Brown ran a business organization out of the church called "The Ethics Group". They did ethics training and their focus was business-to-business. So after my temper tantrum and yelling at God, I called the Reverend (a man *of God)* and get this...he became a client. I laugh at this because at one minute I was yelling at God and the next I was doing business with God through the Dunbarton Fairport United Church. Go figure! Do you believe now? **This success tip is to have a belief...be it in what you're doing and in God or a higher power.**

Tip six: Another success tip is to ask. Never stop asking for business or for help. Just keep asking. I have developed an attitude now that if I don't ask, I won't get. I don't care if they say *no*. The reason we don't ask is based on our fear of rejection. But understand that when someone says *no* it's not personal...it just means *no*. You put meaning into that word...trust me you do. But realize that *no* might actually mean *maybe, not right now* or *convince me*, as well. If you take *no* personally you might not hear these other meanings and you'll lose an opportunity.

I remember hearing no from a prospective client when I was cold calling and I heard my mom in my head...oh man...she came in loud and clear and gave me this bit of career advice, "David, see...I told you radio wasn't meant for you." That voice in my head was my own inner critic trying to trip me up but I wasn't buying. I kept going...remembering that *no* might not mean no *forever*. Perhaps when you hear someone say no to you it's just because they don't know enough about you to be able to say *yes*.

So your job as a good little marketer is to get permission to continue to market to them and to educate them on the benefits of what you do. Got it? *No* means *no* or it means *I don't know enough about you just in this moment to say yes to hire or retain your services...*

The 6th tip is to **ASK no matter what. If you don't ask you don't get—plain and simple.**

Tip seven: My next success tip is to have balance. Hey, I know being in business can get away on you. There's so much to do in the early days, but whatever you do make sure you schedule time for the other aspects in your life that are totally important. Balance the key priorities: family, health and your friends.

Just keep your schedule clear during your prime working time. For me my prime working time is from 8 a.m. until 5 p.m.—that's when I work. *After* or *before* that work period I leave time for my workouts at the gym...and yes, I go three times a week. Make time for your family or you will be living a lonely life and also make room for social time too.

Some ways to plan for balance include scheduling things into your planner and simplifying things. A big project can be accomplished in bite-sized pieces. Also negotiate for time with your clients. Often a deadline has some room to move. So **success tip seven is having balance...**

Tip eight: Lastly, look at your clients or potential clients not as sales but as new and awesome people to have a great relationship with. Can you imagine if the service we got at a store was based on this idea? If the girl at the checkout counter looked at all the customers as friends and as people to have a relationship with, what kind of service could we expect?

Look to build relationships. Nurture your clients, add value to your relationship, dine out with them once in a while, get to know them more personally and you will soon see that you have loyal clients referring business to you.

So my last tip is to **build relationships with your prospects and customers.** Like a marriage, relationships take time but can be so sweet.

You can accomplish a lot with nothing. Don't let money, or the lack thereof, stand in your way.

MODIFY THE VISION

You might have a big vision, that's great, but sometimes you have to modify the vision. You just might have to scale back—at least for a little while, especially when you are just starting out.

For example, you might dream of opening a retail gift store but with that comes a lease, inventory, advertising costs, heat, hydro, phone, Internet, packaging supplies—the list of your costs is as long as your right arm.

So, you've got to ask yourself if you can afford it all. And if you just can't then scale back, start smaller, consider a joint venture—team up with someone else who might be open to sharing their space and contacts; they might even be open to sharing the costs of your start-up.

I worked with a business owner who had a big vision to open a gift store but the costs and the challenge of finding a good location were big obstacles to overcome. This client had money to invest (about $35,000) and could obtain financing at a bank but when it came down to the concept for the store or the kinds of gifts she'd focus on she drew blanks.

The coaching she got was to scale back. I suggested she begin smaller. I advised her to begin with a gift basket company that she could run out of her home and steadily build a client base. Once that client base hit a critical mass *then* she could begin to look for a location for her clients to come to.

A home-based business was still along the lines of her

vision but the expenses and risk were much lower. She would have the ability to "grow" into the big vision over time without risking her assets and possibly her confidence.

You see having a vision isn't all just airy fairy stuff...it's about tapping into your own inner wisdom to know how far you want to go. Take baby steps, know your risk tolerance, have a plan and set little goals along the way.

If you're driving from one end of the country to the other you don't expect to get there immediately. You make the trip in bite size chunks, stopping along the way, enjoying the trip and all the towns, the scenery and the people.

WORKSHOP

Ok, it's time to do some work...

1) How can you create time for more balance in your life?

2) Who can you get to help you with the various aspects of running your business that you don't really have a passion for or care to do?

3) Who can mentor you?

4) When will you have completed these three things?

DEVELOP SUPPORT SYSTEMS

Your business should be a part of your dream not your nightmare. All too often our dreams get shattered and one of the key reasons for this is we are too afraid to ask for help from others. Jack Canfield (life coach and co-author of the *Chicken Soup for the Soul* book series and a class act) suggests in his teachings and books the importance of asking for help or for what you need. I agree. Here is a post I wrote a few years ago and I hope it helps you get started.

STOP AND ASK FOR DIRECTIONS ONCE IN A WHILE

Blog Post, August 2009

> As good as it is to begin your business with a vision, please don't forget to stop and ask for directions along your journey...
>
> I have learned that successful companies and businesses hire help. No one person can do it all. It's that simple.
>
> The challenge for a lot of small business owners is that we feel we have to do and manage everything. Yes..."If I don't do it...it just won't get done properly." Sound familiar? It should...it's what we think deep down inside most of the time. We like to micro-manage our businesses to the point where we are driving ourselves crazy. We've become great at multitasking—taking on way too much.
>
> Work and business shouldn't be about taking on way too much. Your work has to be an expression of what's inside you: your joy, your passion, and your true gifts to the world. It has to be about wanting to make a difference in the world. Yes...ultimately it's about building a better mouse trap.
>
> But even that mouse trap takes many hands to build and market. You need a designer and a manufacturer. Someone has to mould it, package it, market it, price it, cost it, sell it and do the back office stuff—like bookkeeping and payroll.
>
> A lot of people go into building a mouse trap...so it's likely that in your business it's going to be the same. Begin to get help.

> Hire in the areas of your business where you're weak; hire out the jobs you just don't like to do. If life is about living your true joy then make it a plan in your business to do what brings you the most joy.

Get help along the way my friends. Here is another article from my blog that reinforces the need to do that and demonstrates the power in asking for help.

GET HELP ALONG THE WAY

Blog Post, July 2008

> This spring and summer have been a great time of change for a lot of us. I mean look at how some of the economic and social realities are forcing us to change and adapt. What I think is happening is that these socio-economic factors are really getting us to focus on the important things in our lives. We are forced to invest in the areas of our lives that matter most. We must become more careful and intentional about where we spend money. We have to be less frivolous and think more about getting value and a decent return on our investment.
>
> But you know change doesn't happen without help along the way.
>
> I mentioned recently about some personal changes I was going through. One change was taking weight off; a second change was reconfiguring my business plan and concepts; and, the third change was personally adapting to those socio-economic conditions that we're all facing these days.
>
> So as to my weight loss, so far I am down 20 pounds...thanks to some dedicated workouts with my personal trainer, Chris. Chris has coached me and pushed me to a point where I am jogging around the gym in between my sets of weights. He even makes me do squats...and I hate squats!
>
> The bottom line is the energy is back, the vitality and the passion...all necessary to run a business these days...

My business is starting to take shape too as the rebranding and new website are oh so close to completion. I have been surrounded by great people helping me along on my journey.

Now study and look at the picture below...because that's us sometimes. We are like little kids needing a guiding hand and when times are good we are the adult...leading the way. We all need the sage or the spiritual warrior who knows the path and can guide us along the way.

photo by Joshi Manjummel

We all need help and as entrepreneurs our downfall is that we don't ask for it. Out of shame maybe? Or God forbid, someone will think we're weak and not successful. Or sometimes our belief is that no one can do it like we can and we say, "I will do it myself!"

I say park those stories and get some help. Train your staff to do what you do. Take on the tasks you like in your business and hand the ones you don't enjoy to someone else. Get the help you need. Ask...ask...ask...get the help along the way.

I got coaching help from Kim and Jacqui at Frame of Mind Coaching around my weight loss issues. The program that Kim and Jacqui designed included weekly coaching calls and journaling on a daily basis. It included journaling our thoughts and feelings around a certain weekly discussion point. In week 7 of our 10 week program we had to journal about "gratitude" and I wrote about a time in my life when I had lost my father. I was 10 years old. He died suddenly...the abruptness of it all left my entire family in shock, depression and wonderment...

It left me without a dad...totally not cool...and I felt like an outcast at school and in life...I mean crap, eh? I was the only 10 year old at school without a dad...

So in writing about gratitude during my 10 week coaching calls Kim reviewed my journal and asked me a critical question about this time in my life. She asked about who my mentors were after my father passed on.

Who were they? I wasn't sure. My first thought was that no one was a mentor. It wasn't my uncles or those closest to me. But then as I wrote my response it became apparent that the people I'd think would be my mentors weren't but my cousins, my brother-in-law and a CFL football player were my mentors. You know it's odd but when you're not aware life supports you totally.

Sometimes if you expect people to show up they don't and that clouds your vision making it hard to see those that do show up and help you along the way. So you've got to lose the expectations you have about and around people and just let life unfold. The lesson I got in this time in my life was that life totally supported me through that difficult time.

And now back to the point I was making about getting help along the way. I hope you've learned some core lessons.

1. **Ask for help if you need it.**
2. **Lose your expectations (preconceptions) of others.**
3. **Trust that the universe is taking care of you at all times.**
4. **Know that the best people will show up if you allow them too.**
5. **Have an attitude of gratitude.**
6. **Realize that you've got to get out of the way--let your negative thoughts, worries and fears vanish and choose positive ones instead!**

BUILD A TEAM

When launching your business venture you need to put a team in place. **Don't go it alone.** A team comes in many shapes and sizes: a mentor, a coach, a mastermind team and, yes, a board of directors too. Let's look back at a blog post detailing who you'd want to surround yourself with in your new venture.

WHO IS ON YOUR TEAM?

Blog Post, March 2010

> This month, I have become aware of the importance of having a team to support you in your business venture. In fact, having a team around you in whatever you are taking on that's big is almost mandatory. If you're having a baby you have a doctor, a gynecologist, your friends and teacher from the prenatal class and so on. If you're trying to take off weight you've got support from a nutritionist, a doctor, a personal trainer and/or the team at Weight Watchers as well.

Having a team is vital to your success. In biblical times, Moses had Aaron, Jesus had the disciples...Noah had a bunch of animals, but we won't go there this time...

The lesson in this newsletter is the importance of having a supporting cast around you to help you run and grow your business.

There are four key types of support in the business world:

The first one is a mentor. A mentor is someone who's in your field, who is successful in the field and is open to counselling you or guiding you once a month about your business and the direction you're taking it. One way to access a mentor is to talk to the trade association that's connected to the industry or field you're in. In almost every industry there is a trade association and what you want to do is ask the director of the trade association who the top five most successful business owners are in your industry. Once you've got that information you then want to call each owner and see if they would be open to mentoring you. Usually when people are successful they are all too happy to share their advice. Why? Because it's something to be proud of and it's an honour to share it!

A good mentor relationship is one that's done over the phone once a month. You have to be respectful of the other person's time. It's not out of the realm of possibility to send a thank you card and a gift certificate to your mentor as well...once in a while. Showing appreciation is always a good thing.

The second type of support you can have is **a mastermind group.** Your mastermind group can be made up of professionals in your industry or it can consist of a variety of business people from different industries. The idea of a mastermind team was developed by the "grandfather" of the personal development movement, Napoleon Hill. He felt the power of five or six minds were better than one. One of the first mastermind groups included Ford, Firestone and Edison...quite the mastermind team to say the least.

When choosing your team you have to be with people you trust, who have the same goals and who can help you get to where you want to go. A typical mastermind meeting is about two to three hours long and it's a chance for you to brainstorm, test, and work through challenges and then get the advice and insight from the four or five other people in your group. I personally don't like a group that's more than six people or the meeting can take all day.

You can make your meeting fun by having a nice breakfast or lunch. You could have a book review, share online resources or best practices. In my mastermind group we did experiential dance that allowed us to get into our bodies. After we danced we created a vision board. My vision board had pictures and words cut out from magazines that resonated with me. I then glued each picture and word onto a Bristol board. My vision board reminds me of what I want to achieve for my life and business.

A mastermind group has to have respect, trust, cohesion and good communication. I recommend you meet once a month to keep the flow going. Your mastermind group isn't about you getting psychological help; it's about getting support, ideas, and action steps that you can take for your business venture. Yes, some emotional issues may come up but remember you are with business people not a psychotherapist or psychologist. Keep the meetings about the task at hand rather than making them more personal.

A mastermind team can be a great support mechanism for you to put into action in your business venture and the ideas and the encouragement you get are invaluable. Heck, you might even get to dance like I did in a couple of my meetings and anyone who knows me knows that I'm no "twinkle toes". But, I did have fun and let loose for a while. Sometimes you need to let loose and play even if it's during a work day.

Another support system to put into place is **an advisory board.** An associate coach of mine, Tanya Geisler, teaches her clients about the power of an advisory board. Tanya leads entrepreneurs to have access to their very own advisory board. The difference between a mastermind team and an advisory board is that the advisory board focuses solely on you, whereas a mastermind team is a shared focus. Log onto Tanya's site and check out the work she does helping small business owners start their own advisory boards: http://tanyageisler.com/board-of-your-life/.

Another aspect of having an advisory board is demonstrated by an experience I had this past week. On Thursday, I met with 8-10 senior business executives and they helped direct me and give me ideas, advice and feedback on my business. I went in totally cold not knowing what to expect. I did go in with some key areas I wanted to discuss and I got 90 minutes of ideas, counselling and advice to put into action immediately. I also became clear about the most immediate next steps to take and engage in.

These 8-10 very astute professionals are part of a very unique organization called A-S-E (The Association of Senior Executives). These seniors have made their living (successfully) and it gives them a chance to be vital, give back and make a difference, plus the advice I got was really very amazing. I paid $90 for 90 minutes and walked away with some ideas that had never occurred to me before. You can check out this service at www.a-s-e.ca .

Finally, as far as an advisory board goes, to quote my friend Tanya when she helps to lead and facilitate an advisory board, here is what's possible: "Imagine a brainstorming session dedicated to your unique values, your particular brilliance, involving people who know you well and will applaud your success. An Advisory Board from your very own life that comes together for one single purpose: to help you land somewhere new—lovingly and safely.

Board of Your Life is not for the squeamish—it's for people who are ready to take the reins of their life and become 'unstuck'. Are you ready?"

An advisory board helps you discover pieces that fit your puzzle.

Our last support system is **a board of directors.** How many of you know what that is? Better yet, how many of you have one? I have a feeling that not a lot of business people have one of these. You are in charge of putting together a board of directors even if your company isn't on the stock exchange. It's vital that you share the state of the nation, as it were, about your business venture.

A typical board of directors consists of your lawyer, banker, accountant and another business colleague. A typical board of directors meeting involves taking these four professionals for dinner twice a year to share what's going on in your business.

Since you've got four very different people at the table with you, you will get very interesting feedback. I feel a good board includes someone with a financial perspective, one from a management perspective, one from a legal perspective and one from a banking management perspective—all with contacts and experience that are crucial to your success. Make sure when you meet twice a year with your board of directors that you take them out for dinner.

Success...isn't that what having support is all about? Isn't that what we all want for ourselves?

WORKSHOP

You have more work to do...

1) Who would you like to have as a mentor? Who do you know in business that can help you and can guide you along in your venture? Here is a tip, ask the leaders in the industry you're in. They can really help if you remember to ask.

2) A mastermind team is a *creative* team that can help you brainstorm, work through business challenges and keep focused on your goals. Of all the people you know, who are the five that you would love on your mastermind team? (FYI, you want to keep a mastermind team to about six people maximum.)

3) Who do you need to meet and have coffee with in order to get information and ideas on how to improve your business or get it up and running? Good research and knowing the market is the key to your on-going success!

PART 2: GETTING IT GOING

In this section, we're going to look at the different types of business structures and how to register your business and begin to legitimize your vision and idea. We're going to make it become a reality. Let's start shall we?

First you need to set the stage. What do you want? Who do you want to be when your business grows up?

BUSINESS STRUCTURES AND LEGAL ISSUES

Before you begin you need to know that there are three different ways that you can register your new business: sole proprietorship, partnership or corporation. It's important to consider the pros and cons of each type of business registration before you decide which one is the right fit for you.

Sole Proprietorship

The first way, the SOLE PROPRIETORSHIP, is the easiest. You can easily start your business by registering with your province (if you live in Canada) or your state (if you're in the U.S.A.). If you live in another country, check with your local government, especially the economic department, to see what the legal steps are that you must take to launch your business.

In most cases you must register your business name—it's a legal requirement. (In Canada if you use anything other than your own name, with *no* additions, you

HAVE to register your business.) I think it's important to register a business name, even if the business is just in your name because it gives you credibility and it makes your business feel real. Besides if you do open up a business bank account or get financing they would want to see that you've registered your business. Lastly, you may need to register for tax purposes and in some cases if you want to join a trade association you'd need to be a registered business owner. I think it's important especially for credibility.

Pretty well anyone can be in business as a sole proprietor as long as the particular job doesn't require special training or a degree. Now if you decide that you want to be a brain surgeon you will definitely need years of med school and a degree behind you. But if you've always baked cakes then you don't need a special degree to do that. You *will* need a clean kitchen and a safe work environment that is sanctioned or approved by the health department in your area, however.

But before you register look at joining an association within your sector or field. There are a myriad of trade associations that you can join and it legitimizes you as a business owner. For example, as a consultant I can join the Association of Independent Consultants in my city. That allows me to learn about my industry, share best practices and also participate in joint venture projects with other business consultants. Good deal.

An industry trade association can help in many other ways. They have group insurance, meetings, education, trade fairs and more. All of these services that an association offers you will help you be better at what you're doing.

These are all good reasons to register your business. You register to make it legal. The first three letters in the word "*leg*al" are also the first three letters of the word "*leg*itimate". By registering your business it also "legitimizes" you. It gives customers the perception that you're a reliable, trustworthy business. Which of course you are, right?

So definitely register your venture (name of your company) with the local and appropriate government body in your area. Look to the economic development agencies to find out exactly what you need to do. When registering your name you want to ensure there aren't other businesses with the same name doing exactly what you're doing. It will confuse the customer and you might get slapped with a lawsuit to stop you from using the same company name that someone else has.

Now if it's the same name and you're in a different geographic location, then you should be okay to use that business name as long as you're not competing. However, the goal in choosing a name is to be original. Here is a hint: try and use your name in the title of the business you're running and registering. If that doesn't appeal to you then have a brainstorming session to come up with a creative name for your business.

One of my colleagues went to a marina, looked at the names on boats and selected two names he liked. People love to name their boats. He wanted a business name that sounded "worldly" and he picked the names Sorenson and Ring...right from two different boats. He then named his company *The Ring Sorenson Group* and that wasn't even close to his own name.

I don't get too hung up on a business name; what I worry more about is the tag line following it. It's in that tag line that people, *your customers*, should be able to know what you do. My business name is *The Technicolour Umbrella.* That may not tell you what I do but when you hear what my tag line is, "Creative Growth Strategies for Small Business", you understand right away.

Let's get back to the registration of your business. As I said, the first and easiest way to register is as a sole proprietor. Almost all of you can do that. You usually don't have to register with the federal tax department when you are a sole proprietor unless you have employees and have to set up a payroll account and/or are required to have a BN (Business Number).

You will file your personal tax return and include the business forms with it when you file your return. I do recommend that you speak to a government representative and/or an accountant/tax preparer so that you understand if you need to register your business, how you should record income/expenses and what you can use as deductions and write-offs *before* you start your business. You want to make sure that you are doing all you need to do *now*, not *later.* Proper record keeping is VITAL. The government has many tax guides to help self-employed taxpayers. Of course federal and provincial/state websites are great places to get information as well.

It is not necessary to register for the GHT/HST (in Canada), in most cases, until the business' gross income is $30,000 in a single calendar quarter **or** in four consecutive calendar quarters. This saves a lot of hassle such as collecting and submitting GHT/HST and having to prepare GST/HST returns. Also, since you don't have to charge GST/HST you can keep your costs down for your clients while you get your business established. (Legally you can't collect this tax if you aren't a registrant; however, the moment you go over the $30,000 threshold you should consider yourself a registrant and begin collecting it.)

Take the time, and get the help you need, to understand the tax rules when running a sole proprietorship. Make sure you understand what you can claim as deductions on your business return. Heaven knows you don't want to overpay and you for sure want to deduct (within reason) all you can!

As a sole proprietor, you are it. You *are* the business. You are responsible for all aspects of the business, good and bad. You are the salesperson, the marketer, the bookkeeper; sometimes you even clean the floors. As a sole proprietor you need to come up with the funds, sell the idea, market the business, nurture clients, have a sense of the bottom line and control of the money. You sign the cheques, file the returns and pay the income taxes.

As a sole proprietor it is important to plan and grow your company with the future in mind. Plan your business so you don't have to be doing everything all the time, 24/7. Creating a business plan can help you focus on where you are now and where you want to be in the future. You don't want to be in the habit of doing it all yourself for too long or you will burn out. You do need to focus on what you do best in your business and hire or contract other experts to help you grow.

The good news is that this is exciting; the bad news is that it can be overwhelming. I cannot stress this enough—plan your business with the view of having a support cast working with you. If money is limited and you can't hire someone full time, hire on a "as per need" basis. You can have a Virtual Assistant take care of some admin work offsite (s/he doesn't even have to come to your office); a bookkeeper or accountant can handle the cash flow and tax issues; and, a cleaner is a nice treat to keep the office in tip top shape. You have to get close to good suppliers, your bank representative, an accountant and even a lawyer and then use them as resources and guides to help you along the way.

You can expect long hours at first, but if you like what you're doing it won't *feel* like work, I assure you. However, make sure you strive for a balanced life style too. Keep an eye on your health, spirituality, family, friends and your social life too so you have a balance to all the work.

While you are mainly on your own financially, there is a new opportunity for self-employed workers in Canada (effective January 2011) to contribute to the Government Employment Insurance Program. This will provide access to EI special benefits like maternity, parental, sickness, and compassionate care. Check out the Service Canada website for more information.

One last point, as a solo-preneur it is essential that you get proper insurance. If you get sick your lifestyle and business are at risk. This is where products like critical illness and disability insurance can see you, and your family, through rough times. Don't forget about life insurance—to protect your family and assets and to cover debts and final expenses in case of your death. As a business owner you should have business liability insurance or errors and omissions insurance. Talk to a good insurance broker and look at your insurance as something that "protects" your standard of living should anything go wrong.

Partnership

The next legal entity to consider is a PARTNERSHIP. There are two kinds of partnerships. One is a Limited Partnership where there is at least one general partner and one (or more) limited partners. The limited partner is just acting as an investor. Usually this is your rich uncle...or a good friend or family member. They invest a set amount of money, knowing there is a risk they might lose it, but hoping to get paid back, with interest.

They don't, however, work in your business. They have limited personal liability for the partnership's debts. (Their risk is limited to the amount that they contribute or agree to contribute to the limited partnership.) You work the business; they only help to provide funding or start-up capital.

The other form of partnership is a General Partnership. This is where two or more people work in a business with a view towards making a profit. Generally speaking, subject to the Limited Partnerships Act, general partners have unlimited liability. Like being in business for yourself, you need to know that in a partnership you are responsible for the gains and losses of a company and to all creditors if the business fails.

Though many of the same things apply to partnerships that we covered in the section about sole proprietorships, there are some additional things to consider. Partnerships present special insurance concerns. You could talk to your insurance agent about "key man" insurance and a buy-sell agreement that would protect the partners in case of a death or illness/disability. It is beyond the scope of this book to go into specific insurance needs but you need to be aware that a partnership structure *has* special insurance needs that you should discuss with a professional. More on that later in the book!

If you decide to team up in a partnership then you have to get a clear-cut partnership agreement drawn up first. There are some important things to consider before having it drawn up. You have to know the responsibilities of each partner—who is going to do what. What are the roles each person will take on in the business? What are the special talents of each person? Who will monitor each partner's spending? What will your dispute settlement procedure be? You must set clear work expectations. It is imperative that you have crystal clear communications to avoid future problems. A partnership agreement will also cover the possibility that a partner may need or want to leave the partnership and will set out how this can be done in a fair and equitable manner.

Keep things on a professional level—*don't*, and I repeat, *don't* treat a partnership like a friendship. You're not friends, you are business partners. Have a clear mission and vision statement. Have a fully developed operations manual. Operate from each other's strengths and focus on those, not on any shortcomings.

I have an unwritten rule in business and it's *never do business with friends and family.* It can become too personal and then you potentially expose yourself to a world of hurt and aggravation. Even though you love each other...working with those that you love does not (necessarily) a good partnership make.

So to sum it up be sure to create a partnership agreement. *Go in* with your eyes open and have an exit strategy so you can *get out* with your shirt intact.

Corporation

The last legal entity to consider is a CORPORATION. This type of structure essentially protects the business owner's personal assets—home, car, savings, etc.—from creditors should the corporation fail financially. Being incorporated isn't something I suggest if your sales are less than $250,000.00/year. The costs of incorporating and running and maintaining a corporation have to be considered.

If you are worried about liability (and like the protection of personal assets that may be available by owning a corporation) don't forget that it's possible as a sole proprietor/partner to use products for your investments that can offer creditor protection. And remember that even if you are incorporated, as a director your personal assets may not always be protected from creditors—be sure to read the interview with Albert Luk that follows.

When you do incorporate you have to use a lawyer to set up your corporation (unless it is very simple). This can be quite expensive. You must also file a separate tax return for the corporation annually, a T2 return, and you will probably require the services of a professional to have it prepared. There are other tax slips and financial statements to be prepared annually as well. Again, this will most likely require a professional's help. Also, a corporation usually has to make monthly income tax installments to CCRA (unless the income is very low or non-existent).

Incorporating can allow you to sell shares, raise funds, get investors, but with each aspect you need to do it legally within provincial or state laws. You can't do a stock offering and sell shares in Canada without getting the blessing of the Securities Commission.

There are two potentially significant tax benefits of incorporation for a small active Canadian business:

One benefit is a tax deferral that is possible when earnings are retained in the corporation. (The net income of a sole proprietorship or a partnership is taxed directly in the hands of the owner; however, a corporation is a separate entity with its own tax rates. You only pay personal taxes on what you earn as a managing employee of the company you created.)

The other benefit is a $500,000 capital gains exemption available on the sale of a small business. (It can only be claimed on the sale of shares of a qualifying corporation and not on the sale of a sole proprietorship or a partnership.)

For more information on the tax advantages of incorporating log onto: http://www.bdo.ca/library/publications/tax/taxfactors/2009-03/tax-advantages-of-incorporating-for-professionals.cfm

There is a lot of paperwork and many costs to think about before you decide to incorporate. I recommend waiting to incorporate until your risk, or sales, are at a significant enough level. It's not necessary to incorporate right away and it can be more cumbersome than beneficial. You have to weigh the pros and cons. This is a big step in the evolution of your business.

I have only touched on a few issues for each of these business entities. I highly recommend you research these more before you register yourself as a business. In Canada you can log onto: http://www.canadabusiness.ca/eng/. This is the Government of Canada's site that can answer almost any question you have about the three legal business structures and will help you to decide which one is right for you. In the U.S. log onto their supersite for small business at http://www.sba.gov/. This site is the U.S. Small Business Administration site and can tap you into a ton of resources and help you access information and money for your venture. In any event, you can always check with your local Board of Trade or Chamber of Commerce for information. Your local library is chock full of information too!

Since we are discussing legal business structures let's talk to a professional. Albert Luk is a business lawyer based in Toronto, Ontario with DEVRY SMITH FRANK LLP and he really knows his stuff. I want you to be totally clear on how to set up your business so you avoid any mistakes. Here is my interview with Albert. He's very knowledgeable and informative as you will see.

Albert, I have touched upon the three legal business types: the sole proprietorship, the partnership and the corporation, but what are some of the legal issues and challenges that each of these business types might face and that business owners should be aware of upon opening their venture?

Sole proprietorship and partnerships are business structures which are easy and cost-effective to open and close. However, on the other hand, they do not offer the business owner any liability protection personally nor are they tax efficient business structures. As a result, the business owner is more exposed personally when utilizing these structures. Any legal liability of the sole proprietorship or partnership will be the business owners' as well. For business owners with sufficient assets to their name, this becomes a concern.

Corporations do offer liability protection, subject to certain exemptions, and are taxed at a lower tax rate. The cost of these advantages is off-set by greater paperwork. Since, as you noted, a corporation is a separate legal entity from the business owner, the corporation will need to file its own set of tax returns, keep its own set of books and its own HST, employer and WSIB numbers.

Let's start with a sole proprietor...in order to protect themselves from any bad business deals, bad clients or poor performing suppliers what legal documents, agreements and information should they have prior to starting?

Regardless of industry, all businesses should have a Sale of Good or Services Agreement which governs the relationship between the business and their customers. It is important these agreements contain strong language about how the business is paid and what happens when there is non-payment. Too often, many start-ups forget to ask for deposits or release the good or service without being paid in full. It is always harder to collect money after you have delivered the good or service.

Anyone doing business with another person should have a Partnership Agreement, for partnerships, or a Shareholder's Agreement, for corporations, which addresses how the parties will operate the business and what happens if someone wants to leave or is asked to leave. A well-drafted agreement will end up saving the parties a lot of time and money in the event of a disagreement.

Businesses hiring contractors and employees should also ensure they have signed Contractor or Employee Agreements. A professional contractor should have a well-drafted agreement for review. For those dealing with intellectual property, the Contractor's Agreement should clearly state who owns the intellectual property being produced/licensed or sold. Otherwise, in Canada, the default is the contractor. Employee Agreements should address issues like confidentiality and how much notice is required to terminate the agreement.

Any business dealing with confidential information should have a template Non-disclosure Agreement prepared. At the very least, it protects a business' trade secrets and shows some deal of sophistication. Please note though that angel investors and venture capitalist firms do not sign non-disclosure agreements; investors deal with so many businesses that they would tie their hands by signing a non-disclosure agreement. Handing them one shows you do not understand their business.

The partnership is similar to a sole proprietor in terms of the pros and cons, but when you have two or more people running things, issues and disagreements can come up. Similar to the last question I asked, what does a partnership have to have in play before they launch—from documents, to

agreements, to any other legal issues that might befall them?

As I mentioned, partnerships should have Partnership Agreements prepared to govern the relationship between the parties.

Lastly, what goes into incorporating, Albert? I see and hear of a lot of business owners subscribing to a "do-it-yourself" kit when they incorporate—to me this is a recipe for disaster as they might not know all of the implications that go along with it. What are some issues and challenges we might have to face when we incorporate?

There is a time and place for do-it-yourself incorporating. However, for many early-stage companies, it is not appropriate. Incorporating a corporation is the act of filing articles of incorporation with the government. However, the corporation will then have to prepare by-laws and resolutions in order to authorize the corporation to undertake certain acts. Many do-it-yourself business owners miss this second step. Since a Canada Customs Revenue Agency audit may include an inspection of the corporate records, it is important to create and upkeep corporate records.

Another important issue in incorporating is the appointment of directors. Too often, a corporation has directors which are not the operators (typically the spouse or family member of the business owner). Directors do have certain personal liabilities acting as a director and, furthermore, can block certain types of transactions from occurring.

I am asked from time to time whether to incorporate federally or provincially. The legal distinction between a federal and provincial corporation is small so there is no material advantage of incorporating federally vs. provincially and vice versa. It is more business convention to have businesses that are regulated by the federal government—pharmaceuticals, telecommunications, and international trade—incorporate federally. Many of my import-export clients incorporate federally for this reason.

Does incorporating really protect us from creditors? Isn't Enron a bit of a case in point?

Enron is a bit of an extreme example but our incorporation regime offers limited liability protection. It is limited in three major ways. Firstly, unpaid taxes by the corporation are the responsibility of the directors personally if the corporation cannot pay the taxes. As indicated earlier, it is important to choose your directors wisely as a result. Secondly, a Director, officers or shareholders who guarantee the obligations of the corporation are not protected through incorporation since the liability is both the corporations, as the primary obligator, and the directors, officers or shareholders in their personal capacity. Finally, incorporation will not protect individuals who engage in fraud, criminal activity or use the corporation as a mask to pursue some personal vendetta.

Having said that, incorporation does shield its shareholders from personal liability to the extent they have not provided a guarantee. Since a corporation is a separate legal entity from its incorporators, directors, officers and shareholders, the liability is the corporation's and not any of those individuals.

What are the advantages to incorporating?

There are two primary advantages. Since the corporation is a separate legal entity from its incorporators, directors, officers and shareholders, it offers liability protection. Secondly, since corporations are generally taxed at a lower rate than individuals there are tax advantages to incorporating. It is important to note though that the money must stay within the corporation in order to take advantage of the lower tax rate. Otherwise, any money paid to the owners is taxed in the owner's hands at usually a higher tax rate. This would also be a good time to mention that the tax advantages to incorporating are best utilized if the business is making taxable income approaching the highest marginal tax rate for individuals (approximately $128,000 in Ontario as of 2011). Most start-up businesses do not fall neatly into operating in high liability fields or with high taxable income which would suggest incorporating immediately. Instead, they should seek professional legal advice to see if they should incorporate.

Albert, changing topics a little, when do we sue and take someone to small claims court?

In Ontario, any claim worth under $25,000 (not including interests and costs) is brought before the Small Claims Court of Ontario. Most businesses begin a lawsuit either to recover monies or to remedy a breach of contract. The more written evidence there is to support or defend a claim, the better the claim or defense. The lesson being: keep good records.

What are the realities of going to court to settle a business matter?

Statistics show that most lawsuits are settled. I have read anywhere from over 95% to 97% of lawsuits settle before going to court. There are four business realities to going to court. The first is time. Most court procedures will take at least 6-18 months to be heard. The second is that trials are 50/50 propositions at best; this is why most lawsuits settle. Someone knows they will lose and so they settle so only the highly contentious cases get to court. The third is recovery. Winning a lawsuit does not automatically mean the victor is paid right away. The victor has to now take proceedings to collect; if the loser has no money, the victory in court is hollow. The fourth is cost. Time is money and lawyers cost money too. Realistically speaking, a business owner has to make an assessment based on those factors to determine whether to sue and, if a lawsuit has been commenced, how far to take the procedure.

What do you urge your clients to do when settling a business argument?

I was once taught that a good business agreement is one in which neither party is happy. In other words, each side gave up something of importance. In other words, be prepared to compromise and trade something of value in return for something of value.

So I have to ask you this...some people say that in today's business world contracts aren't worth the paper they're written on. What's your take on this?

I would beg to differ. It is not that the contracts are not worth the paper they're written on but it is that the parties do not have the political will to enforce the terms properly. A well-drafted condition is not only about what happens if you do not do something. It should ideally govern how the parties will behave even before there is a default.

Albert, as a small business owner having a lawyer can be a bit expensive, but it's necessary. What do we want in a lawyer and what areas of the business does a good lawyer help us with?

Fit is a high priority. You can hire the best lawyer in town but if you do not get along with him, how useful is that? Competence, obviously, is important but it is not just that they understand the law but that they do understand your business. A lawyer who acts for real estate developers is going to have a harder time understanding a tech business than a business lawyer who has a stable of tech company clients.

In terms of areas of law, lawyers are your out-sourced risk management department. Begin with conversations about risk management. Lawyers being gate-keepers and connectors are also good sources of referrals to other professionals and individuals.

Thanks Albert. That was very informative.

Now that you have a better understanding of the three legal business entities (and possibly have registered your business) let's delve a little more into what's required to run your own business.

CREATING A SOLID FOUNDATION

Is it possible to do what you love and for your business to be an expression of joy and passion?

Let's see!

BUSINESS AS AN EXPRESSION OF JOY

White Paper Report, June 2009

One of the coolest case studies I have been exposed to in my business life was from expert marketing mind Tad Hargrave. Tad has a beautiful marketing consultancy practice that's changing lives. He works predominantly with business owners in the healing arts and green business industries. He talks about designing your business to be an expression of love and joy.

At first as I read his article and musings, I thought to myself, "Yes, but my parents used to say, 'Nose to the grindstone, no pain no gain…if you work hard you'll get results.'"

Then as I continue to read, what Tad is talking about begins to settle in…this is truly what our work must be about, if we're *really* going to succeed. Work, or our businesses, must be an expression of our passion, joy and love. The questions now become: How do we make that happen? How do we design our business so that it can be about joy, passion and love?

How can we create a buying experience for our customers where that is the feeling we are orchestrating, each and every day?

Here's an example of how being in business can be an expression of joy. It's the story of Dr. Paddi Lund. If you go onto his website http://www.paddilund.com/content/view.asp you will read about the radical changes he made to his dental practice so that going to work, and the patient experience, became all about joy. You will also read about his success secrets:

"Dr. Patti Lund is The Crazy Australian Dentist!

Crazy? Because in order to improve his sales he actually:

Pulled down all his signs and locked his front door,

Took his name out of the phone book,

"Fired" more than half his customers,

Sawed up his reception desk and installed a Cappuccino Machine instead!

Now bakes fresh dental buns for clients, and

Serves 30+ varieties of tea in fine bone china.

Yet now also ...

Only accepts new clients 'By Invitation'

Works 23hrs/wk & earns 2½ times the income

Loves going to work & is really happy!

Dr. Paddi Lund has completely redefined the customer experience, successful sales techniques and referral marketing. Read and hear all about how Paddi did it - including step-by-step how you, too, can improve sales and, like Paddi, mix business, happiness and profits!"

Paddi wrote the book, "Building the Happiness-Centred Business". It's a paradigm shift. It's belief altering…but it works.

It has caught the eye of many expert business minds including Jay Abraham, perhaps one of the leading marketing minds in business today. Jay is a well-respected Californian marketing guru and head of Abraham Publishing. This is what he wrote about Paddi Lund:

"A lot of people talk about paradigm shifting, changing our belief systems, etc. But this man is the definitive expert on the subject. If happiness, liberation control and financial security are important to you, study these books. They will change the entire way you look at your life, business and value systems.

I've always been impressed with Paddi, and his story is a model I've used to demonstrate three different ethos: 1) Revering your value to yourself and the value that you bring to others. 2) The power of playing life by your own game and your own rules. 3) Having a hell of a lot of fun in the process.

I admire what Paddi has done with his life. I admire what he is trying to do to help others." (Abraham, Jay. "Business Experts Give Their Acclaim." Web, 7 February, 2012 <http://www.paddilund.com/content/view.asp?name=DrPaddiLund_WhatOthersSayAboutPaddi#JayAbraham>.)

What about other examples of joy at work? Tony Hsieh, of the online clothing retail store Zappos, has created a whole culture on Delivering Happiness. His new book and website (and now a movement) encourage other business owners to incorporate a higher level of customer care and satisfaction into their business. Delivering happiness to customers *and* employees really becomes the focus.

If this notion of delivering happiness gives you meaning and I know I love the concept, then log onto www.deliveringhappiness.com to learn how your venture can be a business that really walks the talk on customer service excellence!

How do *you* bring joy and passion to work?

I say it's all in the balance. You've got to live a life of balance. You've got to take care of you before you can really take care of your customer in such a superb way as in the examples above. So where do you begin to get that balance?

ALWAYS HAVE BALANCE

So what do we do when those New Year's goals don't quite take shape the way we want them to? Now I know you are scratching your heads, saying to yourselves, "He did say New Year's *goals*, right, and not *resolutions*?" Yes indeed, I did say goals. Personally I don't like resolutions, they are too short-term to me and chances are they get broken within a week or two, right? Yeah, you know because you've made a few and broken a few in your lifetime. So have I.

So, goals seem to me to last longer. They are long-term. I mean if you take a hockey player or a soccer player who scores a goal, they last so long that they go into record books and onto the back of hockey cards. So goals are long lasting.

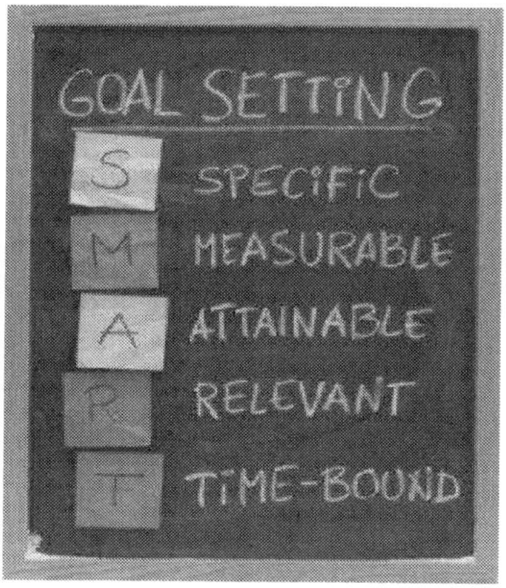

This New Year coming up, I say *resolve* to set *goals*. Goals have to be SMART too. By SMART I don't mean that it's a comparison between silly goals and smart goals (perhaps a silly goal is the thing you need to motivate you this year). When I say SMART goals, I am referring to goals that are **s**pecific, **m**easurable, **a**ttainable, **r**ealistic and **t**imely. You can look at the goals you are setting and know that you can actually achieve them; there is a measurement to each goal and it's possible for you to achieve it and do so in a timely fashion.

TAKE "SWIFT" ACTION

You see, when you make goals you want to tip the scales of success in your favour. I love reaching my goals and so I set them around the five cornerstones of my life. I take a holistic approach to goal setting. In fact, I call my holistic approach the "SWIFT" method. I set goals within this framework so that all aspects of my life are in balance.

To me, my life is based on:

S...is for SOCIAL. One of the social goals I set out to accomplish each year is to go on a blind date, for example. Yes, I am single and want to meet that certain special someone. Another "SOCIAL" or "S" goal is to have a party with friends and another one is to go see jazz concerts...these are definitely attainable goals...and they're fun too!

W...is for WORK goals. Being in business I want to work on my website, get two new accounts, and develop a new brochure within these next few months.

I...is for INNER. This involves prayer, meditation, reading, learning...as Dr. Stephen Covey says, these are the things you do to "sharpen the saw" so to speak. Some of my "INNER" goals include prayer and meditation.

F...is for FINANCIAL. Oh yes, I want to pay down my debts like anyone else and contribute to my retirement savings plan too this year...pretty honourable financial goals, huh?

T...is for things in life that need TAKING CARE OF. Those mean health, family and yes, my Weight Watchers meetings.

When you combine these core areas of your life I believe you are beginning to live in balance. So what do you do to keep these goals in sight and what can you do to encourage *you* to stay focused? My recommendation is take it all on, live life full out, play by the "SWIFT" method...but divide the tasks up *and* into categories and headings.

The next step is to assign the necessary tasks to accomplish the goals and address the issues in each area of your "SWIFT" list. I do this on a large piece of Bristol board and use 3M Post-it Notes to write down each action step I need. On the Post-it Notes are the tasks or goals. Once completed, I remove each note and put up a new task that needs to be done.

The Post-it Notes act as big reminders for me and give me focus. On each note are the actions I need to take in each area of my business. The Bristol board can be decorated and fun. If you want, you can include motivational sayings and pictures as decorations and to help keep you motivated during the lean times.

Once you are refocused on the tasks you need to take in your business, you start to feel good because you are always in action around key areas of your business. And trust me...when you are in action, those results will come! So work on creating your "Action Board". It's amazing what can happen when you think about things to do in your business, write down your goals and actions and see it in front of you every day. I use a board similar to this and I find it keeps me focused.

On the next page, I have an example of an "Action Board" for you to see what I am talking about. So don't get panicky about resolutions—set goals around the areas that really matter to you this year. Just take action and stay in action. You will love the results!

Social	Work	Inner	Financial	Taking Care of
Go on dates	Develop contact list	Attend prayer services	Meet my planner	Book Sundays for family day
Have a party with friends	Meet 10 new clients/month	Read 10 minutes a day	Set up a budget	Go to the gym three times a week
Go to Jazz Concerts	Call at least 10-15 clients/day	Do Yoga and meditate	Invest 10%	Do the cleaning

As you can see above, the chart lists each key goal or task. Use Post-it Notes so that once one task is complete you can remove it and identify another task, goal or action step.

But balance in your life or business is more than just good planning; it's also about having a sense of contribution. It's about giving back to society, to make it whole, just and fair. Don't do this if it's not in your heart and you've got an expectation. Do it if it fits your lifestyle and schedule, if you have time and can make a difference.

WORKSHOP

1. What are three goals in each category of your life that you can work on this next month or two?

2. Who can hold you accountable?

3. If you have managed to have a day where all key elements of "SWIFT" had occurred, what did

that day feel like for you? How did you feel about yourself at the end of the day?

GIVE BACK TO YOUR COMMUNITY

Sometimes in business you've got to follow the basics. One of those basics is giving back to the community. In this day and age, it can't be all take and no give. I mean just witness some of the big brokerage houses in the United States that folded, due to excessive greed and mismanagement.

Here is a blog post about giving back.

THE POWER OF GIVING BACK

Blog Post, December 2007

Happy Holidays! I wish you my very best wishes for a healthy, abundant and joyous New Year. Making it great...that's my motto for the year ahead.

One way to make it great is to volunteer...on December 5, 2007 the world celebrated International Volunteer Day. It's a way to recognize volunteerism. In Toronto, CITY TV staffers were involved with building a house for a family in need through Habitat for Humanity. Recently, I gave up a couple of hours on a Saturday to help prepare a meal for the homeless. My good associate and business woman Gail Hutton takes time out of her business life to spearhead this event that helps the homeless. She feels that in life you have to have meaning and by volunteering she finds that meaning in helping others.

Personally, I have been a mentor to a young entrepreneur and am on the Board of Directors at my place of worship. I have helped the homeless, raised funds for the Kids Help Phone, coached individuals, made phone calls, walked the Terry Fox

Run a few times...the bottom line is when I volunteer, I get to enrich my own life.

I remember when I was with the Kids Help Phone Foundation. I assisted them for five years. I was in the promotional products business and met a ton of contacts through my work with this foundation. I enjoyed doing that more than networking to be honest.

When I volunteer I feel a connection to others and that I am making a contribution *and* I am networking, believe me. Only the networking isn't forced...it's natural. People you volunteer with get to see the "real" you—a "you" that has time pressures, assigned tasks, ideas, and that offers a helping hand.

If we are really going to make a shift in the world, it starts with us. Helping each other...making a difference. It's about community. We're already hearing the phrase "buy local, shop local". We want to make our communities stronger and volunteering is a good place to start.

A rule of thumb though, you need to get involved with something you're passionate about. Make sure you involve your business associates. My good associate Shawn Shepheard lets us all know about his involvement with Team Diabetes. He is a diabetic and the guy is a hero in my books for having run three or four marathons for that very cause. Believe me, Shawn lets everyone know about this charity and the work he's up too.

You may also find that going to those monthly networking sessions isn't bringing you much joy; there is no better place to network than at an association you're lending time and energy to.

As you look ahead, choose a charity that you want to become actively involved with and volunteer; it makes good business sense. You might ask why. Well, the networking you can do while you donate your time is one reason. The other is that you can take your skill set to a new level and bring that back to the business you run. Lastly, if you promote your involvement with a charity and let your clients know it really puts you in a different position in the minds of your customers. You are now part of the community. You aren't just taking; you're giving something back.

Companies now are encouraging their staff to volunteer too. It brings forth better camaraderie at work, it unites the team, and it helps to retain employees as well.

The facts are there, believe me. When you volunteer, it brings you a wonderful feeling to know you've given back to your own community. If you are a company that gives back and believes in contribution to the community, it will do a lot to improve employee morale and build your teams at work. It fills the soul.

In my religion (Judaism) there is a standard by which we live. It's known as TIKKUN OLAM (teak-oon-olam) and it means *to mend the world*. To make the world a better place while you are here. I live by that philosophy in my work and in my volunteerism. It's a good feeling seeing a project get completed too.

In the New Year, commit to volunteering and watch your sales and business improve vastly.

COMMIT TO BEING A BUSINESS THAT LOVES TO LEARN

Successful companies are companies who know how to keep up with the times. They keep informed and they know that their employees also have to stay informed and on top of their game. Companies that invest in training their teams usually reap bigger rewards professionally and financially and it boosts morale! This blog post explores this concept further and why successful companies have a *learning* mindset. As you move forward in your venture you've got to commit to learning, to reading, to asking questions. Your success will depend on it! If there is something you don't know how to do in your business or you need to improve on your skill set, learn about it. They say good sales people are born not made...hogwash! They are born but of course they are made too. They just learn and adopt good lessons perhaps with more zeal and energy than others do.

This is a case in point about how important it is to learn and become a student of the game of business.

Let's go to school shall we?

COMPANIES NEED TO HAVE A LEARNING MINDSET

Blog Post, September 2011

Each September, as the Labour Day weekend ends, there is a new energy. It's about going back to school or getting back to work. It's a refocusing time. In September, I was asked a question by the *Toronto Business Times* magazine. They asked, "When you're in a small business, where time and money are key factors to consider, what steps would you take to establish an employee training program?"

My reply was that as a business coach and facilitator this is a great question, because it's one I face in engaging my clients. When I am pitching sales training or team training, it's often tough to get people to commit the time. When promoting public training programs where a small business owner has to be away from the office and the "busy-ness" of running a business, it can be tough as nails, so to speak, to get a solo-preneur to take a day to learn. So as someone who works in the learning and development field this is a question or an objection I come across regularly.

So how do you overcome this challenge?

If you're in human resources for a large company or if you're a sole proprietor, the key is that you must be scheduling training into your business calendar. In this day and age of constant change and unforeseen challenges in the marketplace you have to be on top of your game. It is in your best interest to have a learning mindset to help you achieve the results you want to see happen in your business or with your people in the organization you work with.

In the book *Leading in Turbulent Times* team learning is mentioned as one of the keys to success. Even Dr. Stephen Covey suggests that you have to "sharpen the saw", meaning you must take time to improve your skills so you can work less, work more effectively and apply new ideas and skills to your venture.

The June 2011 issue of *Profit* magazine featured the Top 200 Fastest Growing Canadian Companies. Time and time again, having a learning mindset and being dedicated to training and development of staff, owners and stakeholders was a key in business success.

Rick Spence from *Profit* magazine writes, "So, growing companies must find the right formula for keeping their most effective employees happy. Increasingly, PROFIT 200 firms are investing substantially in their employees' professional development. By offering various forms of skills training, they're keeping their top talent challenged, engaged—and around." (Spence, Rick. "The 5 winning strategies of high-growth companies." Profit. 1 June 2011. Web, 9 January 2012 <http://www.profitguide.com/article/28256--the-5-winning-strategies-of-high-growth-companies>.)

You must work learning into your calendar. You also want to be strategic about it. What kind of training is going to help you the most? Where do you need to improve? What skills need polishing up?

Even though I work with clients to grow their business, I would encourage everyone I work with to really get clear on their needs as far as learning, growth and development go and then begin to seek out the appropriate people to help their team.

One other point to remember is that training and development in this day and age of technology don't have to be in a classroom. If time is an issue then you can encourage your team to take time to learn from home at off-peak hours via a tele-class or webinar or even provide a CD to play as they drive to work or to their appointments. One of the wonderful options in tele-training and webinars is that the organizers can record these so if the timing of the live session doesn't work with their employees' schedule then they can tune in at a later date at a time that's more convenient.

I love hosting tele-seminars. I find them a great way to learn and you can do it in the cozy surroundings of your home, cottage or office! I also love using CDs or downloading information to listen to as I drive, work out at the gym or go for a walk. I can listen as I do these other activities and it's kind of fun taking care of my health as I work out and listen to some compelling training material on my iPod or in my car.

So my advice is to schedule learning and team development each month, then look at time saving options like tele-seminars, webinars or other forms of online learning; and lastly, and this is an important point too, you might want to link some kind of incentive to the learning. I like certificates of achievement that show that team members have completed the training to improve their skill sets.

I used to work in the promotional products association for several years and the association established a credit system that allowed promotional products specialists to obtain their CAS or MAS designation. If you became a "Certified Advertising Specialist" or a "Master Advertising Specialist" it was a designation you would put on your business cards, website and letterhead. It showed your commitment to excellence and in some cases it was that very commitment and level of professionalism that would get you the business.

So here is to your success—now go learn something!

WORKSHOP

1. What organization does your business want to get behind?

2. What can you offer in the way of volunteering? Is it time, money and/or expertise?

3. When will you get started on volunteering your time?

4. What are your learning goals this year?

5. What workshops do you need to take in order to be a better business owner?

6. What do we want our employees to learn so that they can be more effective on the job?

PART 3: MARKETING YOUR NEW VENTURE

I love marketing; it's the part of the business that's fun to do. The goal, of course, is to get your prospective buyer's attention, build their interest in your products or service offerings and get them to buy what you have for them.

But, how exactly do you do that? It's not easy, but here are some ideas that you can put into play. I am beginning the discussion on marketing with some ideas about customer service because it's one area of the business you can easily manage. It's the one key advantage of being a small business that we can totally kick "big business" in the shins on.

Let's get to it!

CUSTOMER SERVICE

Where has it gone and why did it go?

This book is about doing business with heart, soul and passion. It's not about doing business the old way. To me the old way is strictly about numbers, looking good to the shareholders, win at all costs, and "damn the competition because we're going to flatten the bejeebers out of them". This book is about doing business with a pure heart with an aim to contribute positively on the planet. This book is about win-win, teaming up with others and collaborating. It's about building stronger communities. It's about looking out for one another.

That's the kind of world I want to see. It's about being *great* to work with and about offering *great* customer service...

To me being "GREAT" is about this...

G—Greet every customer kindly.

R— Respect each customer.

E— Engage each customer; ask questions; start a conversation; and, understand the client.

A—Have an awesome "can-do" attitude.

T—Thank the customer...a letter that's handwritten wins big points.

So show of hands (figuratively speaking), when you go to a store or do business with the larger companies, do you get this level of service? Probably not, right?

Some of my favourite examples of companies that excel at the game of customer service are: Pike Place Fish Market in Seattle; Mitchells Family of Stores clothing stores in California, New York and Connecticut; and, the McKay envelope company in Minnesota.

I interviewed Jack Mitchell several times on the radio show I do and he was one of my favourite people to interview. He was always so cordial and personable. He took time to refer to the little things in our interviews (such as the Toronto Blue Jays baseball team) that made the interviews more relevant and localized for our listeners. Jack knows how to build wonderful relationships and really pays attention to the little details that make a difference to those he works with. At Mitchells Family of Stores you will find customers come into each of their clothing store locations (Mitchells in Westport, CT; Richards in Greenwich, CT; Marshs in Huntington, NY; and the newly acquired Wilkes Bashford in Palo Alto & San Francisco, CA) for a new suit, but also a hug because the customer is *it*. It's the only reason Mitchells Family of Stores exists. Like Bob Mitchell states in the documentary *Leading with Kindness* it's about the golden rule: do unto others.

I also interviewed Jon Christensen who wrote the book *FISH!* a parable about the customer service approach that Pike Place Fish Market takes on. He is also the creator of the FISH! Philosophy. "The FISH! Philosophy is a set of simple, practical tools to help you create the work culture you've been looking for. It's a way to build stronger relationships that equip you to face your challenges more effectively. The FISH! Philosophy fulfills the most basic needs of human beings who, in turn, fulfill the needs of the organization—more connected teams, better communication, extraordinary service and higher retention." ("Welcome to the official home of the FISH! Philosophy." Charthouse. Web, 13 February 2012 <http://www.charthouse.com/content.aspx?name=home2>.)

Harvey Mackay whom I have talked about already has a business relationship tool called *The MacKay 66.* It is a questionnaire with 66 questions Harvey MacKay asks each client. He will ask customers everything from where they went to school, to their birthdates, to their favourite sports. Why? It's about having deep personal relationships with each client. It's about knowing a client so well and treating them so well that the business relationship is transcended beyond business.

Remember that Harvey MacKay sells envelopes—nothing sexy about that product is there? So service is the only area where we as small business owners can differentiate ourselves. It is the one area we can win at and we can control.

So customer service shouldn't be sloppy and messy, just simple and clean. "Do unto others..."

Here is my blog post on the marked decline in customer service. I hope you enjoy it.

CUSTOMER SERVICE

Blog Post, October 2007

> Is it just me, or are you noticing the same thing in the business world these days?
>
> Lately, I am finding people I am doing business with to be really kind of funky. The networking group leader I used to network with is out of contact with me. The paralegal person I hired to do some work for me never calls me. My own financial agent never checks in to see how I am doing. Prospects you call, and finally get to speak with, don't return future calls. It's all kind of mind blowing sort of, isn't it? A former VA (virtual assistant) just dropped me like a hot potato without warning and checking to see if all was okay before she did that.
>
> Now I don't want to come across like I am complaining, but wait a minute...I am complaining. What happened to common decency, courteous service, a friendly phone call once in a while, a word of encouragement even if the answer is no? Especially from those in larger companies when as a small business person your livelihood sometimes depends on your success with the bigger organizations. Just a phone call to say no or to at least let us know where we stand, so we don't waste our time calling, emailing and embarrassing ourselves.

Let us small business owners have some dignity.

Where did that all go to?

Aretha Franklin once sang, "R-E-S-P-E-C-T". A little respect would be nice, huh? Are we just too busy to do that? Or are we too wrapped up in our own world of concerns and priorities?

You know this week on the radio show our guest is a wonderful guy named Jack Mitchell. He's the author of *Hug Your Customer*. He runs five clothing stores in Connecticut, New York and California and he runs them based on the philosophy *customer first*—treating people so well that it feels like a warm hug to them.

When was the last time you got that kind of service? A thank you card from a supplier, a kind word, a lead, a helping hand, it just doesn't happen so much anymore. I think it's time to offer good service again. I think it's time to make people our priority—to nurture relationships instead of just going after the dollar.

Want other examples of these kinds of companies? I go to a local car dealership and I get to test drive a car for a day or two. When was the last time someone trusted you like that?

Here's a story about a store that I used to visit. They sold automatic thermal massagers (beds) and encouraged customers to test their beds and enjoy a free massage. Free! You were welcome as often as you wanted to come—no pressure to buy. The company philosophy was based on love, kindness and health, really amazing business principles, huh?

What about the free massage thing though? You might wonder how giving something away for free could help your business. Well, eventually the customer will buy the massage bed or belt or perhaps will tell other people and they'll buy some of the products.

Love, health, kindness, trust, respect—stores like these are leading the way.

Now I am not suggesting you give your car away to some guy that walks in off the street, but what about incorporating random acts of kindness in your business? It goes a long way believe me.

Here are some things you can do to beef up your service level this year...

1) **Be grateful no matter what.** Sometimes the people that cause us the most grief in our lives teach us the most important thing about ourselves. From a customer service point of view, thank your tough customers (or send a basket or send a card now and then to one of your clients who may be in pain with a life issue). Do something to pick the other person up.

2) **Return all calls...even if the answer is no**. From someone who has a business selling products, I have to tell you how frustrating it is when I give a courtesy call to see if it's time for you to reorder and then I don't hear back from you. Have some courtesy and return a call. What is one minute out of your day to acknowledge a call, say thanks for the offer and then politely say, "No, not just now"?

   I know if I *didn't* call a client or prospect I would lose the business...so return all calls. You never know when you might have to rely on that vendor again or when the tables will be reversed one day and it's you making a call that isn't returned.

3) **Connect with your clients once a year** to review where they're at and where they want to go. In other words, do a "needs analysis" once a year.

4) **Have some fun with your clients.** A few years ago I booked tickets to see the Royal Canadian Air Farce at holiday time. It was the New Year's show too...so it was an even better show. I took my radio advertising clients and

they got a chance to connect and meet one another. It was fun, interactive and free...not bad, huh?

5) **If you mess up...do something about it.** I messed up with a client this year (yes, it maybe happens more often than that and more than I care to imagine perhaps). I asked them as a way to correct the problem if I could make good on the error and also donate something in their name to their favourite charity. They loved the idea and so did the Sick Kids Hospital.

6) **Be kind first.** Gosh...it's such an insane world these days it seems. Wouldn't a little kindness to others go a long way? It's funny, I was walking the Nature Trail in Ajax on Sunday, October 21 after my show was done. It was a gorgeous day...temperatures in the early 20s. As I walked the trail I was so delighted that about 80% of those I saw along the trail that morning said hello and good morning...WOW...did that blow me away. In my experience, it's unusual to get that kind of response from strangers, especially in the bigger cities, but it's amazing how such a little thing can make you feel so good!

7) **Give back to community.** You know we all have challenges these days: money, health, an aging parent, our kids, the environment...take time out to give back to the community. As bad as we think we have it...there is always someone who has it worse than we do. So give back a little. Donate food at Christmas, lend a hand to the Out of the Cold Program...help out at the Kids Help Phone, walk for a disease or volunteer to help a fundraising walk.

8) **Slow down for 10 minutes a day.** The world will go on without you even if you take a few minutes to relax. Your job is safe. I mean, if the job you do is really that stressful ask yourself who on earth would want it anyway? You might be more irreplaceable than you think!

   So slow down for 10 minutes, breathe, meditate, do some yoga...but take a break from it all.

You know with the end of the year coming soon, we can all resolve to be a little nicer to those in our lives. We all can learn from them, even though at first it doesn't appear that way and who knows what value and richness they can bring to our life.

WORKSHOP

1) What are three things you will do in your business to offer excellent customer service?

2) What will you do to stand out from the competition?

3) If I was to ask your best client one year from now what they thought of your business, what would they say?

ONLINE SOCIAL MARKETING

Online social media...is it the true answer for your business?

SOCIAL MEDIA MAY NOT BE THE ANSWER TO YOUR MARKETING PLANS

Blog Post, May 2011

Mark Zuckerberg wasn't *Time* magazine's man of the year in 2010 for nothing. He's revolutionized how we market, communicate and do business...but you have to know the game of using online social media platforms before you really engage in them.

I am one of the few that doesn't like online social marketing. I don't think it works very well—it takes a long time to get results and it's not that effective in terms of getting closes and business.

I am a big believer of using online social media to educate and provide information that people can use and will find practical. Most of what I send out is helpful, educational and informative.

Maybe, I don't use it enough...but then I am on Facebook a lot and I use LinkedIn and Twitter sometimes. Other than people wanting to follow me, I don't get a ton of conversion—business or sales. However, although this isn't my favourite way to communicate I am a man of the 21st Century and I realize that online social marketing has an important place in business now and in the future. With that in mind I have researched and found the best tips for you that can improve the odds of your business success.

I just watched a video featuring Neal Rodriguez. He's a smash mouth, in-your-face guy from the hood who's rude and crude, but he's bang on about online social media. To quote him, "When I work social media platforms professionally for myself or on a client's behalf, a required byproduct of the activities I perform will produce revenue. In other words, if you don't have an online social marketing strategy and one that has a built in ROI (Return on Investment) then it's just a hobby."

Check out Neal's online rant. As I said it's crude and loud, but he's bang on. It's on YouTube too (go figure). Here is the link: http://www.youtube.com/watch?v=z_wr6gFeh28

You want to make sure that you're not just using Twitter, YouTube, Facebook and LinkedIn (the big four in my estimation) for socializing. Successful business owners don't have time for just socializing. You want to be building your email lists and your community to actually engage, subscribe and pay for your goods or services.

I was looking at some of my business associates' and friends' profiles and when I look at what they post it literally scares me to death from wanting to work with them. Why? Well for starters, they post really unflattering pictures. I don't want to see one of my colleagues in a bikini on her trip or my friend who looks like he's half in the bag. He's a top notch marketing mind—the picture doesn't reflect that.

People, this is what I am saying, if you're on these social media sites to promote yourself or your business you have to be smart about it. Post things that are in keeping with the business image you want! Be mindful of the content you're posting. Is it relevant? Does it make someone get what you're doing and want to do business with you?

Is your online social marketing reaching the people you want it to? Or are you hammering away at your usual list of friends and contacts? If you are already connected to a person on one social media platform, why do you need to be connected to them on another? (And sometimes even a third one?) Why on earth do you have to be connected to them on Facebook and LinkedIn? You've already established a contact with them—one platform is enough! It can all get to be too much sometimes.

STRATEGIC MARKETING

So if you really want to be more strategic about your online social media campaigns, here are some things that you should consider...

1) What's the image you're sending? What is the image you actually want to get across? What do you want to convey to people? Watch your image. I suggest no more pictures of you in a Speedo, buddy. It's TMI, TMI (too much information).

2) What is your core message?

3) Who is your targeted audience? Not everyone on your list is going to buy from you. Focus on the clients you really do want. Who do you groove with? What industries, sectors or groups of people do you love to *work with* and *work best with*! Get

focused and watch the "spray and pray" marketing approach!

4) Have you considered joining groups and tapping into associations online instead and connecting within these social media sites? At least a group or association can be more targeted!
5) Do you know what you want to achieve from an online social media campaign? How many clients, click-throughs, subscriptions, sign-ups are you aiming for—and yes, quantify it in terms of money. Nothing wrong with making money online!

6) Do you know that you can't do it all? Do one thing well and then move on to the next platform. I was advised that I should be on YouTube, sell videos of my workshops, have a different page on Facebook, really use Twitter and get to know LinkedIn.

   The thing is it's too much for me to take on. I am in *social media overwhelm* so I want to focus on two or maybe three things right now and once I have mastered that, I will move on with video, selling things online and tapping into some other new social media technologies. My advice to you is the same one I'm applying to myself—take time, master one and then move onto the next.

   Each social media platform has so many elements to it so take time to really get clear on just one at a time.

7) Are you building your list? To build a list you have to reach out and cultivate business relationships with people—in person!!!

8) Have you asked for permission to connect with (potential) clients? I don't know about you, but I feel like I am inundated with messages, emails, events, things to do, people to see, places to go...ARRRGGHHH!!! There is only *one* me to go around and I have other things on the go. I can't be everywhere at once!

   Ask permission to market to someone, because maybe, just maybe, they are inundated with stuff in their email box and don't even have time to read your material.

9) Are you staying on message? Focus on the benefits of your offering when marketing to clients on social media sites.

10) Are you continuing to build one-on-one *personal* relationships? These personal relationships come before any online social media networking and marketing. A good eye-to-eye conversation with a client is the best way to connect. Why? Well, the eyes don't lie and it's so easy to hide behind the veneer of the web.

11) Are you neglecting other marketing methods? It is *not* all about online social media. Don't forget to use email too...services like Constant Contact enhance your email marketing. Email can bc sent directly to the exact person you intended it for. Also build your email list too. You really want to build your list strategically. You don't want to be a spray hitter if you're planning to hit it out of the park. Keep your focus.

So, those are a few ideas and tips to focus on when it comes to marketing your business online.

MORE MARKETING

Over the years of hosting my radio show (Small Business Big Ideas Show on Radio That Doesn't Suck and online at http://www.rtds.ca or http://ww.radiothatdoesntsuck.com). I was really fortunate to learn from some of the best marketing minds in the business. One of my favourite guests, on my very first radio show, was Tom St. Louis. We both were nervous, I believe, but our interview was compelling.

Tom, as it turned out, studied with the best minds in marketing, Chet Holmes and Jay Abraham, for example. The marketing concepts these two men came up with are absolutely stellar! You've got to learn from them too. I'm going to share a few of the concepts that I have learned from them below.

Concepts like increasing your business incrementally. Think of selling just 10% more products to 10% more clients 10% more times a year. When you do the math and times $1000 in annual sales by 10 customers a year buying once a year and then increase each category by 10% you get a compounded growth in sales of over 30% without having to spend a lot more money.

Another concept is being aware of what your targeted client wants to hear. Knowing that only 3% of the world's population is buying what you've got and another 7% is seriously thinking about buying what you have in the next short while...that means 90% of the population/market isn't interested in what you have just now. So when you market your products or services focus your message on the 3% and 7% that really badly want what you've got.

What will you say in your marketing messaging to those 10% that will get them to say "Wow...I want to know more"?

Chet Holmes talks about educating the client in your marketing message to differentiate yourself. He talks about focusing your marketing efforts; he talks about positioning yourself differently from your competitor. He focuses on your unique value proposition.

Read up on Chet Holmes and Jay Abraham. My friend and colleague Tom St. Louis did and he's blessed me with ideas that he's learned from them.

Here is another article from a White Paper Report I wrote. It's about being competitive in any economy. This report is filled with practical ideas that can help you manage and grow your business venture and start off or shift into a new gear effectively. Enjoy the read!

MARKETING CONCEPTS THAT MATTER

White Paper Report, June 2009

> There is another big issue when you are starting up a small business—finding money. Finding money is always a challenge. There are two really good television shows, one in Canada called Dragons' Den and one in the U.S. called Shark Tank, and they are shows where would-be or existing entrepreneurs pitch to high level investors looking for money for their businesses. In fact, launching a business is no small task. No matter how big an idea you think you have, it still takes a lot of work and a ton of cash.

So these aspiring entrepreneurs pitch their business concepts and products to a panel of business moguls who have the cash and the know-how to make it happen. They've all been there themselves so participants better not walk into the Den unprepared. It takes more than passion to convince these boardroom giants that an idea is worth their attention. The Dragons are ruthless and rightly so—it's their own personal money on the line.

For those reading this article and that do watch Dragons' Den or Shark Tank, what is the number one reason business owners fail to get some "Venture Capital"? Any guesses?

It's due to lack of proper market research.

MARKET RESEARCH

Market research is the collection and analysis of information regarding consumers (potential customers), competitors (same business type), and the effectiveness of marketing programs (i.e. direct mail marketing, newsletters, signage, etc.). It's an *act of action* before leaping into a business and an educated move that determines the feasibility of a new business.

Through market research small businesses and corporations can test interest in new services and products, improve customer service and develop competitive strategies. Both startup businesses and established businesses need to define, evaluate, and plan a course to pursue their market. The end result of market research is creating a business that is more responsive to customers' needs and this, in turn, increases profits.

I love the ideas that author and business expert Chet Holmes talks about in his book, *The Ultimate Sales Machine*. Research done well can actually place your company in a much better position compared to your competitors.

Instead of using the hard sell, use facts, figures and data to educate your client. It's a much different approach to take in your overall marketing messaging initiatives.

Here is a case in point that Holmes mentions in his book and material. When he was contracted to help grow the business and sales of a leading consumer calendar manufacturer research was done that helped to propel sales for that calendar company into the stratosphere. What Chet Holmes' marketing company uncovered was simply brilliant! They tested sales at Wal-Mart versus a leading bookstore chain. They found that sales for calendars at the bookstore chain were far greater than sales at Wal-Mart. Why?

Well, the calendars were positioned at the checkout at the bookstore and consumer studies show that calendar sales are an impulse buy and more of a "point of purchase" decision. At Wal-Mart customers had to venture through the store to the book section to find the calendars. Walking through a big Wal-Mart store is too much work for the average shopper to do resulting in low calendar sales.

So they asked Wal-Mart if they could reposition the calendars at the front of the store by the checkout. Can you imagine what happened to the bottom line? Sales took off big time. A *little* bit of research goes a *long way* toward small business success.

Here is one last tidbit. Wal-Mart outsells a lot of bookstores on books. They carry fewer titles obviously, but they outsell on quantity. That's because Wal-Mart attracts way more customer traffic than many bookstores and when their books sell, they sell well.

Research is the key to small business success. Not only to help improve sales when you change where you place your products (such as the calendars) in your store, but as your business develops market research needs to be an ongoing part of your business. Anyone who is familiar with writing a business plan knows how unpredictable the market can be.

Three essential areas of market research to consider include:

1. **Consumer Research**

    - Information from and about customers
    - Feedback on the likes and dislikes of customers
    - Which services or products consumers like best

2. **Competition Research**

    - What works and what hasn't worked for your competition
    - Ideas you can you borrow from the competition, some call this R and D…no not research and development, but Robbing and Duplicating. Whatever you call it…it's wise to model yourself after successful businesses in your field.
    - Provides insight into how to increase your market

3. **Environment Research**

    - Economic
    - Social
    - Political forces

All of this information shapes the way people do business. Keeping it close on hand allows you to stay abreast of and respond to particular trends or events that influence your small business.

Secondary research sources are easily obtainable. This is information that's been collected by someone else. Google, the newspaper, magazine reports, government data and trade publications are all good sources of secondary research. Don't forget directories like Scott's Directories to help you connect to your best clients too. In case you are not familiar with Scott's Directories, they are business directories that list every business within a specific geographic area. They break down the listings by industry and area, and they list contact names, business size and revenues too. It's a Canadian company and here is the website link: http://www.scottsinfo.com/.

Most forms of secondary research information are accessible at the library or by researching the Internet. Your local Chamber of Commerce can help too in providing data and secondary research.

While all that is helpful, it's actually primary sources you're really after. Firsthand information obtained from your customer or the competition is current, thereby making it the most valuable source for market research.

Two of the biggest showstoppers that small business owners have in compiling research are time and money. If you really don't have the time, find it. Schedule Monday mornings as research days. I personally have never liked selling or calling on clients on Monday mornings and my bet is you don't either. So visit your library and read to *sharpen the saw*—schedule time to research once a week.

Don't forget to hire a student. College and University students are thrilled to get a chance to work in the real world before graduating. It pads the resume and they do great work. Talk to the Dean of Business and ask for some help in research…especially in obtaining primary market data.

We've established a need to do research and we've tried to ensure you've got the funding equation sorted out, but there are still more keys to success that you should use.

Sell *more* to your *existing* clients

Getting more revenue from your current customers is usually a low-risk, low-cost strategy. You could offer incentives on volume purchases, target existing clients with new products, create a website to provide value-added information and/or develop a loyalty program that rewards customers for repeat business.

Remember that McDonald's totally broke sales records when they simply asked, "Do you want fries with that?"

Find new client segments

Is there a market segment you've overlooked? Say, for example, you *currently* sell organic skin care products to women; maybe there is a market for men as well. Focus too on the markets you want to work with. Become expert in them, so that you can "talk" their language and position yourself as an expert. It's better than pitching your goods and services blindly. If you actually are well versed in the nuances and challenges your client segment has and are prepared to meet them then you can watch your bottom line sales increase.

Expand your geographic sales area

My website is getting hits now from all over the world—wild, huh? I am located in North York, Ontario and I have statistics on my website to prove I am getting interest from abroad.

Tap into those markets. One cool way of doing it is to subscribe to "Google" news feeds about your specific industry. Google will email you articles from all over the world about your industry. If you follow up on these articles with a media release and an idea that lends itself to the thoughts and ideas in these articles you may just grab yourself some media coverage in markets that go well beyond your own borders.

If you have been successful selling in your existing market, you might consider opening a new location. Remember though to take into consideration that you are entering a new market place and your potential return on investment could be affected by the high costs and risks of entering an unknown region.

Increase profit margins

Is there a gap between what you're charging and what people are willing to pay? Or can you reduce costs while holding sales prices steady? You may be able to identify a potential revenue growth opportunity. If you just sell 10% more this year, watch your sales take flight. Careful now, let the client give you the budget and price they want before you commit to a price—you may just be leaving money on the table.

Team up

A strategic alliance, such as partnering with another business to cross-sell products or services, can be an excellent way to expand.

Purchase a competitive or complementary business

Perhaps if you own a café then purchasing the magazine shop next door could be a perfect fit, if done properly. While this is a complex strategy and you need to be cautious of which business to buy, the payoff can be high. Consider seeking professional advice to understand your options and avoid potential pitfalls.

Get the help you need

Smart business owners are getting to know the power of teams. Remember what we talked about earlier. Get a board of advisors to guide you along the way. Or develop your own mastermind team. Be sure to get a good group of five to six really progressive colleagues who are team players and will contribute willingly to your mastermind group. (Check out the "Who's on your team?" section if you need a review.)

EVEN MORE MARKETING

Everything you do is marketing...how you answer the phones, how you dress, what time you show up for meetings, what your business cards look like and even your office décor. Marketing is all about the messages you're sending out to people. What does that orange tie you're wearing say about you? What about the fact your desk is a mess? Or that you're consistently late for meetings?

You see, as Marshall McLuhan said, "The medium is the message." (McLuhan's work is viewed as one of the cornerstones of the study of media theory.) It's totally true, even in today's times. *Whatever* you're doing, wearing, communicating, sending out, talking about...it's *all* marketing.

So you've got to be aware of what messages you're sending to people and ensure that you're using the right tactics to get those messages out. Lastly you have to be aware of the strategic impact of what you are doing at all times.

Strategy is your guide. Tactics and messaging are how you orchestrate client perceptions and how you obtain responses from your client base. For example, earlier in the book I wrote about Paddi Lund the dentist, Jack Mitchell of Mitchells Family of Stores, and the Pike Place Fish Market...their strategy is about leading with love and kindness...the marketing and the messaging support the strategy.

Do you think since it's Mitchells Family of Stores' strategy to hug their customers that they would air a commercial slamming their competitors? No possible way...they would air a commercial that spoke about the value and elegance of owning a new suit. They would talk about how important it is to be *your* best and how good it feels to be in a beautiful new suit to wear to work. Mitchells Family of Stores' strategy defines all they do.

What is your business strategy? Look closely and think about it. To me, I believe business strategy is about perception. What is the perception you want your clients, stakeholders and suppliers to have about you?

If you want to be world famous like the Pike Place Fish Market, or have a dental practice based on love or have a company like FedEx based on reliability then you've got to really stand behind what it is you want to be and do everything in your power to be that for your customers and to communicate that in your marketing mix.

Your marketing mix is the combination of what you choose to use to advertise and market your business. The textbook definition of a marketing mix consists of where your business stands as far as *Price*, *Place*, *Product* and *Promotion.* How you price, where you locate your business, what services or products you offer and where you promote really tell the story of your business.

Are you a high end car or a low end car? If you're high end then you would use a more upscale media choice to reach your desired market and promote your product.

Is your product high quality? Or is it low quality? Is it a fad or something that will stay on the market for a long time to come?

Where are you going to sell your product? What place? Is it a low end retailer or a high end one? Is it through wholesaling or online? What's the image or the view you want others to have of your product or service?

Lastly, there is a 5th "P" not included in the "textbook" marketing mix and to me it should be. The 5th P is *Positioning. Positioning* is about the views and impressions customers or potential customers have about your business, service or product. You want to be top of mind when it comes to your customers, so when they need the services your company provides they think of you first.

Companies like Coke, Kleenex and Heinz Ketchup mainly focus on positioning. They want their customers to only think of them. Case in point, Heinz Ketchup's slogan was, "Once you've tasted Heinz there are no other kinds"...they are so well ingrained in our thoughts and minds that when it comes to buying ketchup you rarely think to buy any other brand. Ask yourself this, when was the last time you bought Hunts, Aylmer or No Name ketchups?

Your marketing mix will really establish your place in the market and will define how others perceive you. Be aware of it as you develop your marketing and business plans.

Now in terms of marketing strategy, I love the lessons I learned while taking the Forum. Years ago I took a cutting edge personal development program called the Landmark Forum. One of the concepts they talked about in that weekend of learning was how we live life. Most of us live our lives based on an antiquated model that teaches that if we ***had*** something we desired and could ***do*** what we wished then we'd ***be*** happy.

The model is **have, do, be**.

However, according to the concepts discussed in the Forum, we must flip the model of living and do the opposite of have, do and be.

We must **BE, DO and then HAVE**.

Be the success (or as Gandhi once said, "Be the change you want to see in the world"), ***do*** the actions that co-relate and you will ***have*** the desired outcomes you want.

It's the same in marketing your business. ***Be*** the thing you want to be and desire, ***do*** the right actions and you will ***have*** the outcomes you desire.

This demands you shift your thinking and requires some trust on your part. It's not easy to give up the control. We all like to have the result before doing the actions needed to get there but *first* you've got to try being in the desired state you want to be in.

There are a number of marketing activities you can choose. There are a myriad of marketing campaigns you can launch and there are a number of ways to communicate with your clients and prospects alike. Just make sure that you think strategy first. Let who you want to "BE" guide you. All the rest of marketing and communication is window dressing.

There are many other keys to good marketing. One of the more important points is to know your audience. Know *who* you're talking to, *what* matters to them and *how* to talk the language that speaks to your target market/audience. Just be sure you talk to your clients' issues, solve their problems and communicate your value.

On that note you must know your value proposition. What do you do to help your customers? What are the results your clients get from working with you? How do you make your clients' lives/businesses better? If you know how you impact your clients in a positive way then you're onto what your value is.

If you save money, save time, reduce debts, clean up

messes, change lives, improve the bottom line then this is where your value is and what motivates your client to buy your services. Your client wants to know what's in it for them. How are you going to impact their lives in a way that's going to really inspire them to take action?

If you can define that certain special something about your business...the *magic* you do for your clients then you're on the way to being able to motivate them to take action. If you're wondering how to find out what it is you do or why your clients buy from you then take time to ask them. Within that response lies the magic and the value of what you do.

So, know your value and know your customers as best as you can...these are two key marketing ideas I want to share with you.

The other key marketing strategy is to really make the customer buying experience memorable. Make it so good that they talk about how lucky they are to be doing business with you. (And they will tell you!! It feels so good to get positive feedback from your customers and that helps you to know that you are on the right track. I know I appreciate hearing it from my clients!)

We've forgotten about customer service. I know I have written about it already, but I can't get across to you enough...when it comes to marketing focus on your customer, know them inside out, know how to connect to what matters to them, learn to build long lasting relationships with them and give them service that's "above and beyond". This is what's going to win the day.

Yes, your website has to look professional and you need nice business cards and good strategic advertising. (You want to mix up your advertising and promotional mix a little and try new tactics.) Remember always test and measure the results you get from any advertising; if it's not bringing you the results you want then you need to ask questions and either a) give it a little more time or b) try another tactic.

So there are some marketing rules you need to follow for sure.

WORKSHOP

1. Who is your ideal client? Why? What are the criteria that go into making them an ideal client?

2. What do your clients get from working with you? What are some "end" results or benefits that your clients get from working with you?

3. Why are the clients you chose a good match for what you do?

4. What are your clients thinking when they need to buy your services? What do you think they expect from a vendor like you?

5. Are there certain niche markets you can call on? For example, you might call on women age 35-55, but within that group are smaller bite sized segments. For example women who are

self-employed, single with kids, or women who are married and self-employed, or women who are single with a career and kids, or women with career, married, kids and aging parents. There are more other kinds of segments within the broader (pardon the pun) target group, so choose which one is best for you and serve them like no one else can. Talk their language, understand their specific needs, help them meet those needs and help to solve their specific problems!

PART 4: SELLING

We're going to talk about the one topic that most small business owners don't like. It's called...(breathe in, okay, now release the breath)...***selling***.

In my consulting and teaching work it's rare that I meet a small business owner that loves to sell. But here is the deal. Unless you have deep pockets to hire a sales agent for your business venture, you are going to have to sell.

But let's demystify selling. Selling is not putting something over on someone else. Selling is not tricking someone. Selling in today's world is about providing solutions, ideas and ways to help your clients or prospective clients. It's about having a conversation with your clients and prospects. It's about asking really good questions to uncover needs and to assess what areas your clients need help in and if there is an opportunity to collaborate.

Selling today is about helping your client turn their current challenges into victories. So you've got to be able to prospect, to engage the client and have compelling conversations. You've got to talk your clients' language and connect with what matters to them. You've got to ask critical questions to uncover needs and you've got to have a rock solid solution to offer that's going to work and help shift your client away from pain and back into pleasure.

The key though is not to put off connecting with your clients. You've got to connect and stay connected because studies show it does take in excess of seven to nine contacts *just* to get a meeting. Once you meet you're looking at a five step sales process.

THE 5 KEY THINGS YOU MUST DO WHEN SELLING ANYTHING

1. **Research**. Research the market; research the client; research the needs and issues in the market as it pertains to your clients...

   Can you imagine getting a cold call like this? "Hey Joe, this is Mike Adams here with People Training Services. With the layoffs your company has been going through we can imagine that morale must be a bit low. What we do is help to build morale, regenerate team spirit, creativity and passion at work. We work with our clients to bridge gaps and to recommit to a new future filled with possibility. We'd love to meet to share some success stories and see how we can impact positively on your bottom line. How is next Tuesday at 2:00 for us to meet?"

   What happened here is that Mike got some inside information about his prospect's recent layoffs and the impact that it might have on the company as a whole and was able to position his services to be of help to that client and ease the pain.

   Researching the market is the key to prospecting success.

   Here is another case in point: a home stager is selling her services and the message is about making a house look nice so that it sells faster. That's all well and good...but I want results!

Well, did you know that houses that are staged get over 9% more on the asking price than houses that aren't staged? They also sell faster as well. This is incredible compelling research to share when having a conversation with a client who's in the market and is thinking of selling a house.

Who doesn't want results like that? My house sells faster and makes more money...this kind of pitch is sweet. It shows you've done some homework and you're talking to what really matters to those you're calling. Find me a real estate agent who doesn't want to make more money? Anyone? Show of hands?

When you know in advance what issues and challenges your clients have and you call with an idea or solution to those problems, how do you think someone on the other end of the phone is going to respond? They are going to want your help pronto!

2. **Prospect**. Don't be afraid to get on the phone and call. Yes, I agree, rejection isn't pretty...but if you don't call you won't know what can unfold. You've got to call and prospect and I for one just don't agree with those who say otherwise.

   Make sure your calls are short. Use each call as an opportunity to ask questions and do some marketing research. Engage the client so you can continue to market to them and stay in touch with them. Keep following up until they sue you or you've got a gut feeling this isn't ever going to work.

The other key point about prospecting is that you need to make it a daily habit…an hour a day maximum…and don't get discouraged. Keep asking, sharing, and educating your clients. Keep sharing ideas, successes and helpful tips with each client. Cold calling is like advertising…it's about "reach and repetition".

Lastly, call on clients you think you have a good fit with. Make sure the clients fit with your "best client" profile and also make sure that they need or are using what you've got to sell.

An ideal client profile is one where clients are open to buy, have budgets, have needs, want to be more progressive and are currently using or have used the goods or services your company offers. Other considerations might be the geography, the demographics and psychographics of your client base as well. Use this rule of thumb: call on those you are compatible with. Call on clients where you feel there is a connection.

3. **Ask questions**. Be ready with really good questions to ask your prospects or clients and be ABL, which means Always Be Learning. I have to quote Dr. Stephen Cover again, "See to understand before trying to be understood."

My first meeting is about getting to know the client better, really determining needs, wants, hopes, goals, challenges and the will they have to change or try something new.

Once I know and understand what a client wants I can offer ideas and solutions that fit, that match the budget and that make sense to the client. I do a "discovery session" or a diagnostic interview so that I know what the client wants, needs and expects. If there is a green light to proceed on both sides then I begin to work on a proposal or presentation.

4. **Present.** Work on a top-level follow-up appointment when you can present your ideas, solutions and quotes in person.

   Make your presentation to the client based on the information gleaned in the "discovery" or third stage. I ask for the sale in the presentation phase too and if I bump up against objections I clear them one at a time and run through each objection until none are left.

   I have a little method for handling objections too. It includes wearing your "HATS".

   H—Hear the objection out. Don't judge it, don't solve it…just listen.

   A—Accept it…it's your clients issue not yours.

   T—Thank the client for pointing it out and ask them to give you ideas to solve the objection.

S—Solve...ask the client for a solution that they are looking for, that way you can decide if this is a fair deal or a bad deal to get into...

Once your objection is complete ask if there is anything else that needs to be resolved before moving to do business together. Then ask for the sale!

I always recommend you present in person, because someone can lie over the phone or perhaps even "shop" you around with an email quote, but when you are in front of someone, the eye contact you make is vital to the sale. The eyes never lie. Plus, if the client is holding back you can ask them to come forward with what is holding them back from deciding. This is where you solve and handle objections!

5. **Commence with the work.** Do the best job you can. Ask for feedback; ask to stay in touch and nurture the relationship along the way. You lose clients because you lose sight of staying in touch.

I will get more detailed about the actual selling process, I will share the 6 step sales process that you need know about and work on consistently when it comes to selling...and although we've shared the 5 critical things you must do when selling we will look at them in more depth in this chapter...but to start, I invite you to get thinking about how you sell and what steps you take to engage with a new client to the time it takes to close and get their business...break those steps down and work systematically on making them.

Analyze the steps of how you sell and really see where you need to improve and get better...each step is equally important in how you attract, develop and retain a client. So where is it you can become more efficient and creative with the 6 step sales process or the critical things you need to do to sell more effectively?

We spend a ton of time chasing after a new client, but we fall short on maintaining the relationship. There is an old joke that goes like this...

A man dies on Friday morning and sure enough he's at heaven's gates waiting to get in. But when he comes to meet St. Peter, St. Peter explains that a big mistake has occurred and he is three days early. Since his time isn't supposed to be up just yet St. Peter has a suggestion...

> **St. Peter: Oh man...you're early dude...**
>
> Man: Now what?
>
> **St. Peter: Well, I suppose we can send you back for the weekend...but I am warning you it all ends Monday morning at 8 a.m.**
>
> Man: Okay, thanks St. Peter...

So the man goes back for the weekend and lands on a beautiful island, with all he can eat, all he can drink, a swimming pool, picturesque ocean views, palm trees, beach volleyball, hot looking women, hot looking men...and he just has a blast all weekend...

Sure enough 7:59 a.m. Monday morning arrives and he's beamed back up to heaven. St. Peter welcomes him back and asks...

St. Peter: How was the weekend?

Man: Oh wow, it was gorgeous! It was paradise! Thanks a ton St. Peter and do you think I can go back there for all of eternity?

St. Peter: Well, no...we need you up here; there is lots of work to do up here...

Man: Please, St. Peter, please...

St. Peter: Okay, suit yourself...

Sure enough the man goes back down...only this time he confronts a totally different scene. Fire, death, decay, famine, war and he sees a guy in a red suit and pitchfork running about and asks him...

Man: Hey, hey, what gives? On the weekend I was here and it was paradise now this is like hell...

Devil: Well, yes, of course, on the weekend you were a prospect. Now you're a customer!!!

So, you get the idea, we treat our prospects wonderfully, but we lose sight of our customers...

CONNECT WITH YOUR CLIENTS

Here is why it's so vital to stay in touch. This article is from a blog post I wrote in late 2008.

GET CONNECTED

Blog Post, November 2008

This month's theme is about connecting. Let's face it, we're all going through our *stuff* these days about the stock market crisis and the global financial crisis. It tends to bring up deep-rooted fears, feelings of insecurity, fear about abandonment, loss, lack and not being good enough. You name it and our *stuff* is coming up. So if that's the case then be sure to take extra time for those you work with or do business with.

You're not alone now; others are going through change, fear, worry, doubt and are wondering about life and its meaning. So now more than ever is a good time to connect to those you do business with or work with. Plan a meeting over coffee—or lunch if you're feeling extravagant—but the bottom line is to connect.

I find this time of year, near year end, is a great time to meet clients and talk about plans for the upcoming year.

Find out what motivates your clients, what drives them and what they think about—get to know them on a deeper, more meaningful level so that when the economy bounces back (and it will) and spending is back in fashion, you have vastly improved the relationships you have with your clients. In fact by taking the time now to get to know them and help them, I guarantee that when things do bounce back in the marketplace you'll be the first place they buy from.

I was attending prayer services this morning and saw a good friend and associate. Sure enough his business is going through challenges and life isn't all that great for him just now. So I put my arm around him and said that I could relate, business was a bit more challenging for me too. I let him know that if ever he wanted to chat, go for coffee and just connect that I am all ears.

We left knowing that our bond was closer and can become more so. You see...in tough times, people need to connect more, have a sense of closeness and community and to feel that they can count on their fellow men and women.

So, if you are not connecting to those business colleagues that matter, you may be missing the boat. But connect out of sincerity, out of a sense of love and compassion for your clients. They say what you give comes back, so if you can give without expectation of receiving back immediate dividends then your business has a built in "insurance" plan for the future.

You can insure that the good things you do for your clients and the team you work with will come back tenfold later on.

I remember during the SARS crisis that hit Toronto my coaching business had pretty well gone out the door. No one was spending. To make matters worse, the second Gulf War had just started and people in Toronto were just a little too panicky.

When discussing my business with my mentor back then, he suggested I offer my services for free. This way I could stay in front of my clients, keep in action and also be remembered as a guy who went that extra mile.

You know, it worked. I did free coaching. It didn't pay off right away, but it did later on after the effects of SARS had disappeared. My clients were happy; they stayed with me and even commented that it was nice to get the coaching at a time that they too were facing challenges.

You see, when it comes down to it what matters isn't the money you make, but the lives you impact. That's the real currency that no one talks about on the news. It's the lives you touch; it's the positive feelings you generate. Studies show that we human beings buy goods and services based on feeling and emotion. Wouldn't it behoove you to sell that way? To generate good vibes and feelings for your team at work or the clients you serve?

I was just at a friend's wedding too this past weekend and was there with my high school buddies. We felt a connection—a closeness and a sense that all was right in the world. Why? Well, because we were together, celebrating, honouring our friendships and honouring the newly married couple.

That is what life is all about. It's about experiencing the "sacred" special moments. If you don't think that that is true for your clients, then I have news for you. Take time out to ask them and check in on them. Generate new conversations... link them up with someone else that can benefit from what they do. Plan to help a charity together...just get "connected" to your clients...and watch the magic happen in your business.

Take the slow times in your business to connect more profoundly with your clients. Work to get close to your team at work or your clients and be darn sure to give back now, because it will pay off down the road. It's when the economy does bounce back that your business will soar.

It's about positioning too. Ask yourself how you want to be viewed in the marketplace. What's the legacy you want to be known for in your life and in your business? How high do you want to go? Then get in motion, take action and give back your time, your sense of compassion and understanding to your clients.

WORKSHOP

1. What are three things you can do to stay close to your customers after a purchase is made?

2. What would you want to find out in an annual client/planning session?

3. Who have you done business with that has stayed in touch with you? How did that make you feel?

MAKE COLD CALLS WORK

So why is there so much fear around selling? When I teach my cold calling classes, I always ask this question at the start of the class, "How many of you love to cold call?" You can imagine the response! Maybe one or two individuals in a class put up their hand. The rest of them hate cold calling. They hate selling. Why is that?

There are two reasons really: we fear rejection and we fear looking foolish.

We fear rejection. No one likes it. But here is the deal—they aren't rejecting you personally. They are rejecting the idea that you're offering because chances are pretty darn good that they don't need what you have at the very time you're making the call.

So, to counteract the fear of rejection you have to understand what a cold call is. Let me preface this discussion on a critical issue I am seeing in the "selling" world. Many authors and business consultants are claiming that you don't need to cold call to build your business. Personally I believe that's baloney. Why? Well for starters, someone once said you can't get a cheque or a signed purchase order through email. I find in this day and age too many of us don't want to connect to our clients. We want to do business at arm's length. A rejection by email is less painful than one by phone.

A sales letter or an email blast is not going to close a sale for you. *You* are going to close a sale for you and you have to cold call or prospect.

But let's look at the cold call differently. My good friend and business colleague Michel Neray (Chief Differentiation Officer for The Essential Message, an online branding firm) begins every call with a conversation. Do you agree? I do. Michel goes on to say that *you* began with a conversation. Your dad had to get your mom in the mood in order to produce you!

So that's all a cold call is. It's a conversation. It's a chance to learn about the client, pitch, ask questions, to uncover needs and to probe.

The key to good cold calling is to "stop" selling anything. All you want is a chance to entice and interest the prospect enough so that they will want to continue to work with you. When I call, I want to interest my client in the possibility of increasing their business. What I ask for is about an hour or so to meet them and discuss their challenges, needs, wants and goals. I am not selling my services on the call. I just want a meeting to see if there is a fit between me and my prospect.

Sometimes the prospecting process can take years before you close a sale. That's okay. As you're working with that prospect you have to be working with at least 50 or 100 more...so your pipeline is always full and transactions are always taking place.

So stay with it. Use the cold call as a chance to excite and inspire the person on the other end of the phone to want to know more about you. Once you've got a bite, ask to meet the client to uncover buying motives, needs, budgets and the client's pain. Ask to follow up with a "problem oriented" solution that's timely, smart and on budget.

If you get rejected on a call, ask the prospect if it's okay to probe a little and use this call as a research tool. I love playing "Columbo" (Peter Falk's character in a TV detective show) with a new prospect. After I get told no I ask the client if it's okay if I ask a few questions.

Like Columbo I ask prospects questions about their business so that I can gather more information about them. Often the *no* I got initially gives way to a possible *maybe*. Asking questions about their current situation, checking their happiness levels, and discovering if there is a possibility to work together in the future are my key questions. The bottom line is I am looking for an opportunity to work together. It might not be at this same moment that I have made the call but I work towards keeping the business relationship alive.

I may get turned down now but once the client is in a better position we can work together at a later date. Then I follow up in a way that the client wants and I stay in touch with him, marketing to him, educating him, empowering him to succeed and creating opportunity to work with me and me with him.

I know in my heart of hearts that I will deliver value to him and do my very best for each client. These follow up phone calls are my opportunity to convince potential clients that this is true.

On this call, what I want to find out is not only what the current situation is and the client's satisfaction level, I also want to know what his future plans are as far as my services go and I want to explore the opportunity to be in on that future sale. I also want to know what's working, who he is working with and if he'd be open to an alternative vendor, because one day, that vendor might fall out of favour with the client and that's when I can sneak in. Use the cold call as a way to begin a business relationship. Use the cold call as a chance to find out more about the customer and use the call as a research opportunity.

You see the bottom line is that you gain more from making those calls than not making them. All I ask you to do is to make calls for an hour a day five days a week and see what happens. Just remember never to call on a Monday morning!

Now, let's look at the mindset many people have about selling. Gone are the days of the slap-happy sales person, patting the client on the back and treating him or her like an idiot. Selling today is about your ability to listen more than you talk. Ask critical questions so you can assess the client's needs better. Selling today is based on understanding the psychology of the sale. You've got to be an astute learner and understand human behavior, personality styles, buying styles, management, decision making processes and much more.

It's an art.

Take time to learn it. Read about it. Shadow a top sales rep. Ask for mentorship. Take sales classes. I have a saying about selling, "You can never take enough sales training courses." Be sure to always be learning about how to be a better sales person.

There is an old saying in sales that states, "Nothing happens in business without a sale being made." It's true! Selling is important so be sure to give it the most respect and detail you can in your business venture and become a master at it.

WORKSHOP

1. What are your beliefs about cold calling?

2. How do those beliefs limit you?

3. What are three new beliefs you can adopt that will give you the confidence to make a cold call?

4. Do you feel that a cold call can be turned into a research call instead and can actually be the start of building a business relationship?

HEAT UP THE SALE

I spent 12 years in the promotional products field and we did some cool things to get in the door of a client. My former colleague, Barry Hults, taught me this marketing tactic and it's one I swear works. Here is a blog excerpt on selling I wrote a few years ago; it will help you heat up a cold call and get your prospect's or client's attention...enjoy the read...

A COOL WAY TO REACH A PROSPECT

Blog Post, March 2004

> I love cold calling...yup...I am the one that puts up my hand and waves when asked this question in a sales training session. But like you I have challenges connecting through to people. What with voice mail and our busy schedules, it's tough getting through to a "live" person.
>
> One way to *warm up* cold calls is to launch *niche market prospecting*. Niche prospecting is an opportunity to create clients by marketing to a group of prospective customers (in an intelligent and somewhat aggressive manner) who want to see

you and/or your salespeople. It's a method that allows you to mine for new clients in a concise and focused manner.

The topic of prospecting is vast and certainly deserving of another look. In this article, we revisit the theme and discuss research to help you develop lists of key target accounts in your own business with some cool and creative delivery ideas for your marketing effort. My clients who have used these methods approach an 85% success rate in prospecting!

I have worked with clients who often tell me they sell to every important customer within their target market. But after we do some research, we find there are many new prospects right around the corner they haven't yet tapped into.

For example, a client of mine was hoping to get new business generated in the corporate training sector. Her sales were flat and she needed to break through the door in a more profound way. After discussing the problems related to this loss of income my client had a choice: she could give up the business, or she could market aggressively to gain the volume back through new customers. This client actually chose the second option, though she believed she knew (and in many cases did business with), all of the major prospects within a 20 mile radius of her office.

Our first step was to see if this was true. Using the Internet, we identified 43 companies with more than 500 employees within 20 miles of her location. We were able to pinpoint the companies that she was interested in approaching and wanted as clients.

Do you know all the key prospects in your area?

I often find that as small business owners we don't spend enough time doing research. We sometimes think we know and sell to all the key prospects in our city or region only to discover after a little homework that we really only know a few and haven't even tapped into the wealth of prospects out there.

To check your prospect IQ, try two search tools to discover the names of the largest employers in your area. I like *Scott's Directory* (though you may find a local online directory listing businesses on an economic development website). Also if you go to your local Chamber of Commerce or Economic Development Office they can present more listings as well.

Target the campaign

Now that my client could identify the prospects with which she wished to do business, she developed a campaign to reach those companies by marketing to 15 contacts in each of several campaigns she ran annually.

The campaign was typical of a well-planned niche market direct prospecting program. The objective was to reach sales management and human resource management of these companies and present the distributor as an expert in team building training programs. We believed all companies who have 500 or more employees would likely have team building training programs for their staff.

A new company copy line was created. "Let's Get Engaged" was printed on letterhead and envelopes just below the company name. Two letters along with two engagement-related products were included. Each series of letters was targeted to the VP of sales and the VP of human resources in eight companies from the 43 companies identified in the research. The letters were delivered two days apart and followed up by a telephone call two days later. We sent two gold foil chocolate truffles in a blue (Birks-like) jewelry box (this represented two gold wedding rings) and in the second mailing we sent a photo frame for that "special" day (of training).

The process was repeated every six weeks until all companies had been contacted. In less than 90 days, this client got to meet 30% of those we sent out mailings to and obtained five new training gigs...

Finally, here are some tips to use when you create the enclosure letters.

- Use short, two-paragraph letters with no more than three brief sentences in each paragraph. Managers have limited time and attention to focus on new promotional material.
- Choose a theme. Themed letters with graphics increase effectiveness.
- Tie the copy directly to the product to be enclosed. The connection can be simple. If you want someone to "look over a new service" then enclose a magnifying glass. If you're going to follow-up with a telephone call then enclose a real working telephone imprinted with your logo.
- Consider including short references. Call your clients to get their comments about your products and services. Create a page of one or two sentence statements from several of your clients. Include their names, titles and direct telephone numbers. (Make sure you get the clients' permission first!)
- Package your presentation. Always use an envelope for the letter and gift-wrap the promotional product with attractive paper and ribbon.

Warm prospects who really want to see your salespeople are the key to sales growth for you and your sales staff. Try this process, it really works.

BE BOLD IN SELLING

You have got to do some key things in order to succeed at selling: do research, be bold and don't think that sales are a bad thing. They aren't. This process demands that you be a good listener, proactive, customer-focused, helpful and have integrity around what you're selling.

Here is an article I wrote back in 2003. It was written after an interview I did with author and marketing consultant, Mark Stevens. I recommend that you get his book, *Your Marketing Sucks*. It's a good book to have on the shelf.

Your Marketing Sucks

Blog Post, 2003

> I interviewed Mark Stevens on the October 19 edition of the Small Business Big Ideas Show I host. One thing that came out of that interview was how important it is to be able to sell. Too often I find new entrepreneurs forget this step as being essential. The word *sales*, after all, has a negative connotation to it. You think of the word sales and then you associate it with a huckster.
>
> In truth, I don't blame you. Sales people have had a hand in creating this image. However, two things have changed that demand that this image be totally revamped.
>
> One is that consumers aren't stupid. We have very intelligent consumers on our hands and they aren't pushovers. They are sophisticated and savvy and they won't settle for a flimflam artist anymore.
>
> The other key change that is dictating how the art of selling is changing is that the marketplace is demanding excellence. You can't fake it anymore. You have to be real with the client. The old slap on the back, "Right this way to our new model, sir" and "Isn't she a beauty?" just won't cut it in today's marketplace.
>
> **So what does this mean to you?** Well, for starters you need to know your stuff. Really research your clients. See what their needs are and then pinpoint a compelling angle with which to approach them and open up a conversation. Most cold calls are made without any knowledge of the customer's situation. In fact, only 5% of all sales professionals ever do research on the client or prospect before calling on them.
>
> **Plan**

The next step in good selling is to plan. Identify perhaps 50 of your most ideal clients and focus on them. All too often we get visions of greatness and think we can conquer the world when it comes to selling. I say stop that line of thought right this minute. Seriously, think for a moment, if you have 50 awesome clients right now could you handle any more?

So make a plan. Identify who it is that would make an ideal client and begin the process of selling to them.

The New Parameters of Selling

Yes, you read right. I said to begin the process of *selling* to them. But, it's not what you think. To me selling is about developing relationships. Think of the lovely guy or girl in your life now. You didn't close on the first date did you?

Probably not, but what you did do was talk. You got to know each other and you got to see if there was a fit between the two of you. Alas, if there was, well Mister and Miss became one and began to work with one another.

How can you enhance relationships? To start, send the client something so you stick out from the others who have contacted him. Perhaps you can send an incentive item, like a mug or pen. Be creative here when sending a gift item and make it be part of a theme. You can send a press clipping that may be of interest, a post card, and an article on a similar company in some far off country. Send something that gets attention and shows you are thinking creatively.

Once The Door Is Open

Call them. Be bold here. Talk to the client about an issue they are facing and discuss ways you can solve this issue. That's where the research comes in. In Mark Stevens' book he mentions a conversation he had with the CEO of Salomon Smith Barney, an investment company—not just *any* investment company, actually a financial *powerhouse*—and in the conversation, Mark basically said to Mr. V.P of Marketing,

"You know, your marketing sucks." Do you think that got his attention? You bet it did.

What compelling reason are you using to cold call? Is there a study you can use to support your case for calling? Is there some information you know about or have obtained that can position you to help the client? Open the conversation with something compelling. I challenge you to discover what it is you do that can be compelling.

Set Goals When Cold Calling

Goal one: Always strive to get the appointment. If that fails, and it might, have back up goals. If you don't get a meeting then ask if you can send printed material that supports your company. Or send a sales letter. Get an agreement to keep in touch with the prospect or client if you don't get a meeting on the first call. Chances are high you won't get a meeting right away, so don't fret; you want to somehow get permission to stay in communication with prospective clients, so when that day comes and they need your services or products, you are at the top of their minds. This dovetails nicely into the second goal...

Goal two: The next goal is to be able to send something like a letter or brochure or marketing piece, but get an agreement to follow up with the client at a later date. I recommend a two week waiting period. *Be sure* to follow up. Keep following up thereafter at least once a month until you reach them and get to speak to them or meet with them in person. In fact, I say keep following up until you are shown the door.

Get The Meeting

Once you have a meeting set take the time to research the client even further by doing what I call a "needs analysis". This gives you an opportunity to really understand the client and this session. It will also provide you with the insight you need to see if this is someone you can help and work with.

I spend time with my clients to understand their needs. I ask to see their facilities and plant if that's the type of client I am meeting. Figure out how you can best serve the client during this meeting and develop a rapport. Walk away with as much insight and information as you can about that client.

Follow Up—Or The Presentation Meeting

Once you have all the information you can gather, you then have a chance to present your case to the client. Your presentation is based on the information you collected in the needs analysis session. You will provide the client with the solutions to their problems and then have a chance to detail why you are *the* company best able to solve the client's issues.

At this point, you should ask for the sale. Don't forget to ask, ask, and ask as *Chicken Soup for the Soul* author Jack Canfield puts it.

Let's get back to the really magnificent example that Mark Stevens shares in his book about how a cold call can be done effectively. Mark had a very unique and gutsy edge to the call too...he actually challenged the client—but it worked. Here is the excerpt of how the call went. It's a great learning point for you to know.

> **"This is Mark Stevens. I would welcome the opportunity to introduce you to MSCO, my marketing firm, and the services we provide."**
>
> Marketing Vice President: "Thanks but we are already well served. I appreciate the call..."
>
> **Mark: "Not really."**
>
> Marketing Vice President: "Not really what?"
>
> **Mark: "You're not really well served."**
>
> Marketing Vice President: "I think I am in the best position to judge that."

Mark: "Respectfully, I have to disagree."

Marketing Vice President: "Look, I don't mean to be rude, but I don't have time to get into a pissing contest. I know you'd like to pitch your firm to me, but there's no opportunity here. So please, if you have nothing else to say, I really have to go."

Mark: "But I do have one more thing to say."

Marketing Vice President: "Which is?"

Mark: "Your marketing sucks."

(Talk about being bold. Now here is where the research comes into play. This is why you have to start to research your client prior to the call. You want to back up your message with credible facts and figures. You want to justify the call essentially and position yourself as an expert who cares.)

Marketing Vice President: "And that very biased view is based on..."

Mark: "On the fact that I'm a client of the firm. A Salomon Smith Barney client for more than ten years and in all that time you have never tried to enrich my experience with the firm—to recommend new investment ideas or to suggest investments in mutual funds—to update me on your fee based consulting division. It's as if I don't count. And if it were only about me, it would probably be just fine for Salomon Smith Barney, but chances are the same is true for most of your clients, the millions of men and women who make you one of the largest financial services firms in the world. The fact is, we are being ignored, overlooked and disregarded. It's not because you don't have the products, services and skills to meet—in fact, to exceed—our expectations. It's because your marketing sucks."

> Marketing Vice President: "Are you willing to come in and tell that to our marketing director?" (Stevens, Mark. 2003. Your Marketing Sucks, New York: Crown Business)

BINGO! Do you get it now? When you are selling you need to be brash and get some attention. Do your research on the clients. Perform a needs analysis to get a better idea of what your clients are going through and then present viable solutions that help your clients achieve their goals and solve their problems. Really get into where the clients are sitting and come at it from an outsider's perspective offering new ideas.

THE NEW WAY TO SELL

The new way to sell is really about building long-term trusting relationships with your clients. It's about relaying the message that you believe in what you do so much that you *know* that eventually you can help these clients solve their challenges.

Your relationship-building techniques are geared to sharing the fact that you can help your clients—that you do bring something different and valuable to the table—that you can solve some issue your clients are facing. Selling is about understanding the clients better. Then you have to do what you have to do to keep the relationship open, honest and real. You must be able to build trust.

Selling is such an art. I see a lot of people shy away from it and are in just fear about what it means to sell. Today, selling is about relationships, understanding others, offering ideas and solutions to help someone get a result they're looking to get.

I have broken selling down to 6 steps...if you work them consistently watch your results soar!

THE 6 STEP SALES PROCESS

We have touched on the 5 critical things you must do when selling. The 6 step sales process kind of borders on what I talked about previously in this chapter, only I am about to go a little deeper. Are you ready? Let's dive more into selling effectively!

In my sales training sessions, I talk a lot about the sales process. I like a 6 step process personally. The first step is research, the second is about prospecting, the third is doing a discovery session, the fourth is working on the presentation, the fifth is doing the work and lastly, the sixth step is about nurturing the relationship so you can develop a life-long customer.

Step 1) Research the market

You have to study the market you are in. Know their challenges, the issues of the day and know how you can help your market overcome those.

Also study how your industry impacts your clients positively! Tap into your industry's trade association. Did you know that almost each industry has a trade association?

You can go to your major library in your area and ask for a trade association directory to look up the proper association for you.

Your trade association offers tips, conferences, trade shows, events and resources about your industry that can help you communicate the value of what you do for your prospects and customers.

So research, get to know your markets needs and get to know how you help them!

In the research step, this is really about a few key things...one is getting to know your prospects and customers ahead of the call. It's about "warming up" the prospecting process. No one likes to cold call, but when you meet clients and prospects ahead of the call, it's much easier to call, follow up and book that "discovery" meeting.

Step 2) Warm up the prospecting process

Ways to warm up the call include some of the things we have talked about already in the book. The key way is to network. Networking is about joining the myriad of business networking groups that are based in your community.

The logical choice group for business networking to me is to join the local Board of Trade or Chamber of Commerce.

In Canada, log onto the Canadian Chamber of Commerce site to access the appropriate Chamber or Board of Trade in your area at www.chamber.ca and in the United States tap into the U.S. Chamber of Commerce at www.uschamber.com

The Chamber is not only a place to meet other business owners but also it can be a terrific resource for information to help you research your venture. It's also the voice or a lobby group that acts on behalf of Small Business owners to ensure the governments are acting in good faith when it comes to legislation, programs and incentives for small business.

Your local Chamber or Board of Trade hosts business meetings and networking events. As you attend and meet other business owners, you get to share your ideas, tips, tools to help others that attend. It's a givers gain mentality you need to have when networking and the goal is to build relationships and have those that you meet be dazzled and amazed at how great you are! In other words look at building trust with those you meet!

There are a ton of networking groups in your area, the Chamber/Board is my first choice, but there are others like BNI, (Business Networking International), trade associations, women's groups, moms in business, men's networking groups etc... the list is long, choose wisely!

Once you meet, network and agree to connect with each other afterwards - the prospecting process or that call to book a meeting is a lot easier than making a cold call. You've warmed up the call.

Another way to warm up the prospecting process is to write, speak, volunteer in your community, just get known for the great work you do and focus on your reputation and helping people before going after the sale at every turn. If you're truly helping others, they will come to you, you won't have to cold call so much. You have literally built a reputation as being someone in the know in your industry and when you communicate that knowledge by networking, writing, speaking, volunteering, I promise you, your reputation will warm up the cold call time and time again!

I am not against cold calling or prospecting - sometimes opportunities arise where you have to talk it up to a stranger. Never be afraid to talk about the value of what you do when you meet someone for the first time.

Value by the way is the sum of the benefits you offer a potential client minus the cost equals your value. Your products have value, your products do something to help someone else. You need to get clear about how your products help someone and what they do to better the lives or businesses of others and be able to communicate that in a prospecting call.

Your services have value too...be clear on how your services helps someone's life or business and be able to articulate that too in a cold call or prospecting call...Do your services save money or time? Do they reduce pain? Give someone pleasure and ease? What is the end result? What do your clients and prospects get when they work with you?

Your other benefits focus on brand and relationship benefits. A brand benefit is when you trust the brand, you know it, you can rely on it, you can count on it. Think of McDonalds and Heinz Ketchup here - they do a great job of focusing on the brand. Even a two year old knows about McDonalds.

If you're new or relatively new in business, when it comes to branding you, you want to first of all have a consistent look, logo and feel to your company, you want to be consistent in what you do for your clients and be consistent in the field you're in.

Great companies have failed because the customer didn't know what they stood for anymore. I think Sears in both Canada and the U.S. needs to re-invent itself and focus on its successes and communicate that time and time again to reinforce a more updated, positive and successful image.

The customer isn't clear on what Sears is up too given the branding and positioning work that Wal-Mart and Target have done to build clarity of the business offering in the minds of the customer.

The last bit of value is about the benefits of the relationship your clients have with you. What do they think of when they think of you?

When you think of Fedex what do you think of?

When you think soft drink what brand comes to mind?

When you think of a tissue to sneeze in, who do you think of?

These companies have done a good job at positioning themselves in the mind of its customers so that when you think of that product or service you have a positive feeling and relationship towards them and that their company is the one you will want to do business with.

WORKSHOP

1) Ask yourself this...What do you want to be known for in the minds of your customers?

2) How can you warm up the prospecting process?

3) What are the benefits of your product or service? Can you list 3?

Step 3) Discovery sessions - that first meeting

Lets continue with the sales process. The goal for me when I prospect is to get a meeting. It's not to make a sale on the phone. Chances are selling something on the phone won't work, but if you can say something that might arouse interest in your prospect on the phone, if you can share how they will benefit from working with you, or if you can share a success story about how you've helped another client and how you would love to help that prospect or customer get the same value or experience, then you've done a great job.

The goal of prospecting is to get a face to face meeting to see what the needs, budgets, wants, challenges, goals and hopes are of your customer.

I call phase 3 of the sales process, the "Discovery Process". I was taught this by Eric and Margarida Laffoley when I first started my business. The "discovery" is about you just going in and finding out more information about your clients and to assess if you can help them and if they are a good fit for you too.

It's a fact finding mission, where you ask critical questions to assess where your customer is at and where they want to go and if you can help them get there.

I liken it to when you go to doctor for your check-up. Your doctor will assess you, examine you, ask questions and then recommend a strategy to help you get better or maintain your health.

The discovery is like this. You examine your customer or prospect and then make some recommendations.

This dovetails nicely into the 4th step and that is when you make your presentation.

Step 4) Make your presentation

You want to ultimately present ideas, solutions and actions your clients can take with you that has their objectives, budgets and goals in mind.

It is in this stage too, that you ask for the sale.

You might hear an objection first too...but that's okay, you still have the customer and an objection is really about something your customer/prospect needs to resolve before they say yes. If your customer objects about money or time or your expertise ask them what do you want, what do they need from you in order to resolve this issue?

If you can offer what they want, do it. But, if you need to think about it...you then get into a little negotiating. When negotiating always hold true to your needs. If you compromise your needs, you can compromise your business.

In negotiations, don't act too fast as you may come off looking desperate. Don't give up anything until asked. Trade off on what your customer wants. If they want a discount, then ask for something in return. For example, I can give you a discount in exchange for being paid up front. This way, you both win.

Finally, when your customer does object, and you have solved it, be sure to ask again, is there anything else holding you back from working with us. There may be other objections that you didn't know about and you have to minimize all objections before you go for the close.

Step 5) Do the work for the client

The next step is about doing the work. This 5th step of the sales process is important. You want to use this step to show how professional you are. Stay in touch with your client, ask questions if you need too, check to see if your client is happy with you and get feedback. Stay professional!

Step 6) Build relationships

Lastly the 6th step is to continue to develop that business relationship. Send a thank you card for the deal, take your client to lunch to get to know them on a more personal level, ask for a referral if they are happy and continue to communicate to your clients.

You can communicate with a newsletter, or by having an event, inviting your client to a networking meeting with you, or maybe even going to a ball game together. The key is to stay in touch with the client, let them know of any sales, promotions and events you're offering.

The bottom line is it costs more to get a new client than it does to keep one!

So warm up the prospecting process...follow the 6 step sales process...and work it...become a student of selling and you will never work for anyone else again!

TRUST COUNTS MOST

Don't downplay the trust factor. People say that perception is everything. In some circles they say that perception is at least 90% of reality. Whatever the case may be, you have to build trust. Your client has to trust that you will come through for him when he needs you.

Recently, I was in a pharmacy at night. I'd had a long day that day but Mr. Checkout man apparently had an even tougher day than I did. He was grumpy. He didn't smile or thank his customers even once. When I got to the checkout, I got bold. "Hey man, why the sad face?" I asked. "Oh, I have had a rough day," he told me. Then I added, "So have I, but you are serving me and it wouldn't be a bad idea to smile even though you have had a rough day. Besides, life's not so bad."

My response didn't change his disposition, but I tell you one thing, I will think twice about shopping at that store. I have basically lost trust in the level of service that I will get.

So what can you do to build trust? Here are some ideas:

- Be consistent in your performance.
- *Vow to wow* your customer.
- Continue to send marketing material to your client.
- Seek to *inform* and not to *sell* in your marketing material.
- When you do *inform* your client then back it up with real statistics and data.
- Be the expert—do whatever you can to become the expert in what it is you do.

Summary

The new way to sell is about being bold, getting attention, knowing your stuff, learning about and researching the customer, asking questions, building relationships, developing trust and solving problems. It's not the old "smoke and mirrors" game it once was. It is an art in a plethora of personal dynamics that you should be proud to learn about and execute. It works. You have to understand business, personalities, how to use psychology and how to use the right words to communicate clearly.

Here is my proposition to you. If your sales are down in your business, and they might be, then learn how to sell. Make a promise to yourself to take a sales course this year.

You've got to reach out and touch someone.

You remember the ad campaign from the '80s that AT&T did? The message was simple: reach out and touch someone.

The fact that we've lost the personal touch in business has been a bit of a bugaboo for me for a while, especially since this "online social marketing craze" has taken hold.

Yes, even I have people following me on Twitter and truth is...I am not that interesting. Sometimes on Sundays I don't shower until I hit the gym and that may not be until the early afternoon, so follow me at your own risk. Plus, I am following people on Twitter that I hardly know. How is someone in the States going to sell me a mortgage in Canada?

I now have over 1200 friends on Facebook and truth is, I don't hear from all of them and a lot I haven't met and I am not sure I have a ton in common with them.

Don't get me started on LinkedIn. Does that even work? Someone wants to connect with you on LinkedIn. That's what my email said. I wonder why they want to. Is it about quantity of people you know or is it the quality?

As I move forward into this New Year, I am choosing something different. I want quality. I want to foster close personal business and professional relationships. I think hanging out online on Facebook, LinkedIn and Twitter is a glorious waste of time. Ok, maybe an hour or two a week, but that's all.
This isn't to say that Facebook and these other social marketing sites don't have benefits. Facebook has connected the world and has become the leading communications tool for all of us globally! But, from a marketing point of view and getting clients and building sustainable, long-term personal relationships, it's not that great.

Why you ask? I believe you know the answer. If you are using these sites, how many hours online does it take to convert these connections/friends/tweets into a paying client? It takes forever and that's if you're lucky. My time on these sites just doesn't yield enough results to make it pay.

So, here is my game plan for the future...you can follow along with me or not...

1) I am going to phone my clients more often in the hopes that I will actually get to see them.

2) I want to have more coffee meetings in person with my colleagues and clients.

3) I want to send thank you cards and really "personally touch" them rather than send an email.

4) I am going to email less.

5) When I call colleagues or clients I am going see how life is treating them.

6) I am going to fill the time I usually waste online by reading a book and learning how to be better at what I do.

7) I am narrowing down and focusing on who I want to do business with.

8) I am going to meditate at night and visualize, rather than visualize my computer screen as I watch what people are "twittering" about.

9) I am going to sell the old fashion way, in person, checking for needs, wants, hopes and goals and providing rock solid solutions.

10) I am going to remember that no one ever cut a cheque or a PO (purchase order) over the phone or online. You have to reach out and touch someone.

I always remember my father saying, "You're to be seen and not heard." Not good advice for a kid who became a radio show host and facilitator teaching small business owners. So my advice to you is to get out there, shake hands, meet people, talk, dialogue with people, be creative about it too! You should be both seen and heard!

For example, when was the last time you had a dinner party or a games night with friends? When was the last time you had a meaningful town hall meeting, or a discussion group at Church, your Mosque or Synagogue. The key to surviving and thriving in these times is to build community and not spend your life online. So get out there and make things happen...and touch someone!

WORKSHOP

1) Who is your niche market?

2) What do you want to know about your clients that will help you relate to them on a deeper level?

3) Who are three business people you want to have a meeting or lunch with?

OVERCOMING REJECTION

One reason selling gets a bad rap is due to the hurt involved in it. Rejection is inevitable, so don't sweat it. Don't make it personal either, because it's not about you. I recently pitched Canada's National Radio (CBC-Radio—non-profit, public) network a concept for a small business radio show. I just got turned down. In a blog post I made just after this experience, I reflected on some of the issues I faced and you might face after being rejected by a prospect or client. It's always recommended that you keep the right perspective and not let that rejection get the better of you. Here are some ways to overcome rejection in a much more proactive manner.

MAKING THE PITCH!

Blog Post, 2010

Well, I just got rejected. I pitched the CBC a radio show idea and it got turned down. There used to be a time when that would really have an adverse effect on me, but not now.

Now, I tend to look at ways to build that relationship further...remembering that someone wants to help you especially after they just told you no. So I probed and asked about future opportunities and where I could have improved on my pitch.

The upshot of it all was that I could still be in the game at CBC radio and get in another way. The suggestion was to pitch being a contributor to other shows, like the Current and or Sunday Edition.

The kind woman from the CBC (Canada's National Radio Broadcaster) said that they get hundreds and hundreds of pitches and maybe 3 make the cut. She was kind in her feedback and encouraging too!

The bottom line is this: rejection doesn't mean it's the end...it means *not now*. It means you have to rework things a bit to give people or your audience what they want. So, when you're pitching business, keep pitching, stay in the game, nurture relationships, ask questions and plan for the future.

Let's delve into handling rejection a little bit more.

If you pitch a business proposal or make a cold call and you get rejected, the best bet is to check your attitude. It's never personal...it's just business. It wasn't meant to be and who knows maybe the next best thing is right around the corner. Now that being said, none of us ever like to be rejected. It hurts. Sometimes the thing we seek is something that is vitally important to us. Sometimes, our future depends on it.

Get in touch with the anger

When you do pitch or present a business idea/solution or proposal and you get turned down listen to the voice inside you. What's it saying? Is it hurt? Is it angry? Is it upset? If it is, then get that emotion out of you. Yell, scream, journal, whatever you do, just get your frustrations out...and really let it out, don't hold back.

I used to scream in my car alone and after about 10 minutes of that I would just laugh at myself for being totally silly. It hurts to be rejected, especially if you needed that sale or client and you're wondering if your business is going to work. Was this the right idea? Sometimes you have to just let it out; let out that anger, fear and frustration. You have to let them go because after that moment of outrage and hurt about being rejected and about 10 minutes of pure screaming, you will experience calm about the situation. That's been my experience anyway—10 minutes of hurt, anger and screaming and then... peace.

So once you let it out...once you dump the anger...begin to shift your thoughts and think of what's next. What can you do to be better next time? This is where it's wise to ask the person that said no to your brilliant idea/proposal/concept or pitch about how you can improve in the future.

It's a good time to ask about other possible ways to engage with the client and see if there are smaller opportunities so you get in on some level. You see, if you close the door in anger it may (and probably will) never open up again for you.

Ask good questions

So be sure to ask the person that said no some questions to see if there is another possibility to continue *some* sort of relationship. I liken it to dating. You might not be a be a good fit for that person you go on a date with but having them in your life as a friend may just be a really wonderful outcome!

So ask the person that said no about staying in the loop somehow. If you do get in the door, even in a small way, you never know when a brilliant opportunity might come up in the future. The key is to be there at the right time...and as Woody Allen once said, "80% of success is just showing up."

When you begin to explore why your idea got rejected, you get a better sense of what the customer wants. So this pitch/proposal is a good first effort. The key now is to do a check in to see what the customer's needs are and based on that information you can tailor your proposals accordingly.

Keep the relationship alive

Ask also to maintain some kind of ongoing relationship with the person, keeping it light, professional and engaging. You don't want to bombard the individual; you just want to showcase your talents and ideas in a light informative way.

Know it's a numbers game

The other key thing about being rejected is that you have to know if you've given it your "best shot". That's all you can do. I remember pitching to Adams Brands about handling all of their promotional products needs. We would have printed anything from t-shirts to pens with their logos on it. I came in second. They loved what I did but gave the business to someone who was offering a rebate discount. I didn't even think to offer that, so I lost the deal.

I do remember giving it my very best shot; however, you win some, you lose some.

With the CBC radio proposal I was up against 250 application/pitches a year, two of which get to air. It's hard to be upset when you're turned down with those numbers circling about. I think I would have been more upset if I didn't have the nerve to pitch an idea.

So, never let fear be against you. Keep pitching, keep out there and keep going. If you do get rejected, seek to build and nurture your business relationships. Sooner or later good things will come from it...

Learn from it

One way to overcome rejection is to adopt a learning mindset. If you're open to learning and doing even better next time then you have a learning mindset. You can stand in judgment about the rejection, the company that rejected you or the person that said no, or you can seek to understand where that no came from and then revise and rework your pitches in the future.
If you learn from rejection, if you adapt to what the market wants and you're open to being flexible then rejection won't be so bad.

I hope this post helps you. I hope you have a ton of rejections because that means you're playing full out. It means you're going to get business coming your way because the more you ask, the more you pitch, the more you know your customers, the more you connect with people, the better your odds of success.

Go make it happen!

SECTION II

This section is dedicated to helping you manage your business more effectively. I hope some of the tips and advice given here help you run your business as a *smooth operation.* We will look at managing the business and managing change in the economy, in society and in our lives. Next we will look at money, how to manage it and how to make more of it. Lastly we will look at our mindset and how it pertains to the overall operation of the business.

PART 5: MANAGEMENT

MANAGING CHANGE

Let's face it, not many of us enjoy change. Change forces us to examine our lives and to make adjustments—sometimes painful adjustments. That can cause us to be afraid. Humans have a fight-or-flight response when faced with fear—our bodies are designed to give us what we need to fight for our lives *or* to run away when faced with a dangerous situation. What is your response to change? Personally, I think change keeps us fresh and relevant. If we view something new as exciting then it shifts our perspective. Here is a blog post that discusses managing the *new* in our lives.

CHANGE...HOW IT DRIVES US FORWARD OR SENDS US RUNNING FOR THE HILLS

Blog Post, March 2003

Change is always on the horizon. As I sit down to write my newsletter (and I only do it every other month) I meditate on what it is I am going to write about. Usually it's what's on my mind at the time...and lately...*change* seems to be on my mind a lot.

Personally, I am looking at my life from every possible angle. It's like I am in the process of a redo, a makeover if you will, and I am thinking to myself..."Self, what the heck...here we go again...my entire life is up for grabs right now and it's going to take everything I have to make some positive moves in my life so that I remain healthy, wealthy and well. It's going to take focus, determination, a positive attitude, vision, a mission and surrounding myself with a really supportive cast of people in my life."

It started back in March when I looked at myself in the mirror at Wal-Mart. "Where did that gut come from...it's not like I really overdo it in the eating department...and darn it if I don't get to the gym three times a week...what is going on with me?" I asked myself. I knew then and there some things had to change.

The tough thing is not to make yourself wrong about a seemingly bad situation. What I mean by this is that although you may be unhappy with where you are at in some aspects of your life, you need to learn not to beat yourself up about the situation you're in but to accept what is and embark on taking the necessary actions to change. You also have to learn not to revert to the behavior patterns that got you into this situation in the first place. It's easy to repeat the past mistakes. Recognize that you may be doing that and stop...shift...change.

So I got proactive. In early April I booked my annual physical. I saw my dentist too. I went to my gym and took the plunge and signed on for 24 personal training sessions...

On April 30 I had my annual physical with my doctor. My numbers are up as it turns out and I must work harder at bringing my sugar levels and my bad cholesterol levels down a bit.

On May 1 I started my 24 personal training sessions at my gym and to date my personal trainer is putting me through the paces of a very high energy workout twice a week and he's kicking my butt to be doing something physical five to six days a week. He's also got me eating better too. We've had eight sessions and my strength is top notch; however, I still have to work on more conditioning and taking off the belly.

On May 6 I signed up for a tele-class series too with a new associate coach friend of mine, Kim Ades from Frame of Mind Coaching. Kim is a very awesome coach and speaker and is on the cutting edge of the work you need to do today in order to bring about successful change in your life and business. She and Jacqui Markowitz are outstanding leaders. They are leading a pilot weight loss tele-coaching session, complete with journaling each day and weekly assignments. Also in April and May I was in the process of reshaping my business and my business plan.

Rising gas prices, the economy and a slight business downturn for me are forcing me to really prioritize what I do and where I spend my time, money and efforts. These are all major issues that a lot of us face today: health issues, energy costs, business success, direction, managing and dealing with never ending change that permeates our lives every day.

An earthquake in China, a cyclone in Myanmar...rising prices...it's all enough to make one totally be on edge. How do we make sense of life when it seems to be out of control?

I believe it starts with us. Each one of us has to manage better and control what we *can* control in our lives.

So how do we manage it all without going absolutely off the deep end? How do we make adjustments to our way of life, our businesses, and our economic model without it being too painful?

WORKSHOP

1) How can you handle change more effectively? What are two limiting beliefs you have about change that you can let go of? What is something positive you can say about change?

2) Change is scary...why?

3) Change is exhilarating...why?

4) When was a time you had to adapt to change that had you worried and did you overcome it? How did you overcome it? Was it as bad as you first thought? What are some lessons about how you've overcome change before that you can adopt now?

MANAGING THE ECONOMY

Sometimes things happen which are beyond our control; we all have to deal with economic change. These changes affect our lives and our businesses. What can we do to get through tough times or, better yet, to use it to our advantage? Find out more about managing money—it is the lifeblood of your business. My blog post from 2010 is still very current and relevant.

MANAGING THROUGH THE ECONOMY

Blog Post, November 2010

As I sit down to write this article, I am still hearing that for a lot of us, "It's the economy, stupid." The economy is playing havoc on our minds. There is a lot of uncertainty for sure. In the U.S. the economic recovery and jobs are the two most important factors that saw the Republicans and The Tea Party come out as big winners. The American people are worried about jobs, money and their economic survival.

Don't kid yourselves either; it's the same here in Canada. We don't want *big* government any more. We want *responsible* government and to say so long to the old boys and fat cats that spend, spend, spend. Just witness what happened in the 2010 mayoral race in Toronto, the city where I live. One of the candidates, Rob Ford, promised cuts in funding, less government, more private suppliers and service providers. One of his campaign slogans was "Stop the Gravy Train" and he promised to cut wasteful expenses and costs in local government. He was elected by the way. We see this theme of *cutting back on spending* permeating the world economy.

So, yes there is (as Shakespeare said in his play "The Tempest") "a sea change" taking place. The economy is shifting. You can count on *not counting on* anything anymore. Change is rampant, things are moving faster and faster, there is more noise, competition, bankruptcies are up and there is a concern about our future out there...and there are no *ifs*, *ands* or *buts* about it.

So what can you do as a small business owner to rise above the recession?

Well, here are five things that come to mind:

Find your niche

The first thing is to find your niche—your sweet spot, a little corner of the market that you can serve in a unique, creative way that the competition hasn't totally exploited yet. Find that niche that you can do better than anyone else and market it to the exact channels you're going after.

One example is what my colleague and yoga teacher Tiina Veer did. She is a great business woman. She's young, passionate and creative. She is a top notch yoga teacher and is a massage therapist. She is also a plus sized woman.

Being a plus sized woman, Tiina can relate to the challenges that other plus sized women (BBW) face when doing yoga—especially their desire to participate in this activity in an environment where they don't feel that they are being watched and where they feel safe.

So Tiina created "Yoga for Round Bodies". Brilliant! She owns that niche. Everything she does is geared to helping Big Beautiful Women—from retreats and counselling to yoga. Tiina leads a wonderful class too and may even branch out to plus sized men too in the not too distant future. Just find me one yoga class in Toronto doing what Tiina does, the way Tiina does it. I can't think of many focusing in on the niche market she is working with. She's a true professional and is also an avid social marketer and you'll find her educating and linking up with her *peeps* on Facebook.

So...find your niche and build on it.

Get into the green

Get into the green. The Green Business is about to take off in Ontario. A recent article in the London Free Press newspaper suggests that the Green Industry is taking a new turn in the Province of Ontario: "The green energy revolution is entering a new phase in Southwestern Ontario. It's progressing from harnessing alternative energy sources to opening manufacturing plants at which the harnessing tools—such as wind turbines and solar panels—are built. And that could spell hundreds, maybe thousands of jobs for the London region, still reeling from a recession that sucked away 4,400 jobs in the last year."

Ontario has a number of things going for it. We have a close proximity to the U.S. and we have a good labour force and excellent infrastructure (roads, transit, and high tech). It's all making us the place to look for green sector investment.
Add to this the fact there is a huge solar power project about to be happening soon. Again from the London Free Press: "Ontario is getting so much attention from European and North American manufacturers it is 'turning heads in other provinces. Alberta is now looking at the Ontario Green Energy Act and feed-in tariff program. What is going on in Ontario is hard not to notice.'

Also, the Ontario government struck a $7 billion deal this spring with Korean industrial giant Samsung under which it will build four manufacturing plants in the province, employing 16,000 people—about one quarter of the jobs permanent." (De Bono, Norman. "Up next: Green jobs." IFPRESS. Web, 11 February 2012 <http://www.lfpress.com/news/london/2010/06/25/14519991.html>.)

Now, I am only quoting what's happening near to where I live, but my gut feeling says that the Green Economy is about to take off elsewhere. Look for your local (Not-for-profit Green or Environmental) organizations, associations or companies and tap into what they are doing.

Even Wal-Mart is making huge tracks in going Green and paying attention to environmental sustainability to cut back on costs and also lessen their carbon footprint and be good corporate citizens.

So if you want to beat the recession, go green.

Go after the new

The other hot trend is to tap into newcomers. Here in Canada new immigrants are ensuring population growth since it's on the decline. Chances are this is a North American phenomenon. In fact, locally in Toronto, immigration has become a very sensitive political issue and a hot potato for our local Mayor. In the short term new immigration is a drain on government social programs and spending, but over time, once new immigrants begin to build a life, there are huge benefits to having people from high priority countries come to Canada.

Like it or not, we need new immigration in order to ensure a positive population trend and it also acts as an impetus for our economic growth. Without new immigrants we would probably have negative population growth. So newcomers are ensuring that Canada stays on the plus side of the ledger as far as population and economic growth go. Those are two great benefits.

For business owners there is an added benefit: newcomers need stuff—household products, homes, cars, etc. They bring skills, know-how and money but they are in need of products, services and skills. As Canada reaches the tipping point with now more than 50% of Torontonians being born elsewhere, this sector is too hard to ignore. Tap into the niche markets of newcomers. You will be justly rewarded.

"There is a 'new Canada' just over the horizon—home to a diversity of skin tones, birth countries, languages and religious faiths unprecedented in the nation's history.

By 2031, at least one in four people in this country will have been born elsewhere. New population projections from Statistics Canada suggest that just half the working-age population will belong to families that have lived in Canada for at least three generations."

Sultan Mahmood is an executive member of the Baitunnur Mosque in Calgary, one of the largest in North America. He suggests that Canada's multiculturalism enriches our social fabric.

"This is enriching our society," says Mahmood, who moved to Calgary from Pakistan in 1992. "We're getting good people and all the good things from all over the world, and I think this diversity has made Canada one of the best countries in the world, and I think Canada will remain one of the best countries in the world because of this diversity." ("Growing foreign-born population to forge 'new Canada'." Canada. Web, 31 January 2012 <**http://www.canada.com/life/Growing+foreign+born+population+forge+Canada/2666075/story.html**>.)

Be excellent at customer service

How many of you know what your clients are passionate about? Do you know what kind of hot dog they like? Do you know their golf score? Or do you know their birthdays?

Gary Vaynerchuk is one of today's hot thought leaders. He has authored two key books: *Crush It!* and (his latest work) *The Thank You Economy*. In this latest book Vaynerchuk reveals how companies big and small can scale that kind of personal, one-on-one attention to their entire customer base, no matter how large, using the same social media platforms that carry consumer word of mouth. *The Thank You Economy* offers compelling, data-driven evidence that we have entered into an entirely new business era, one in which the companies that see the biggest returns won't be the ones that can throw the most money at an advertising campaign but will be those that can prove they care about their customers more than anyone else.

I mean think about it, today's world moves so fast. If you're at a night club or bar and you get bad service chances are you're texting your friends on Twitter and Facebook urging them not to go to the club you're at.

Negative experiences, online social networking, fast thumbs to type and a cell phone with all of the amenities equals potential bad press if you, the business owner, step out of line at any given time. That means you have to be at your best at all times!

The Thank You Economy suggests that the businesses and brands that harness the word-of-mouth power from social media, those that can shift their culture to be more customer-aware and fan-friendly, will pull away from the pack and profit in today's markets.

If you aren't putting the customer first you're going to lose out.

Case in point, I was at a well known donut franchise located near the Rogers Centre. I went in needing change for a $20 bill so I could feed the parking meter. The clerk at this location told me no—no change without buying something.

Okay, fair enough…I told her I wanted to buy a *country bit* for $0.25. She refused to sell it to me. "But I am buying something," I replied. She refused again. Not only that she left the counter and went into the store room and shut the door behind her. She left—refusing to honour my transaction!

She finally came back out and agreed to the business transaction, but it was under protest. She yelled at me as I left that she would never do that kind of transaction again. I phoned the head office of the franchise to complain. They took my complaint but never followed up with me to make things right or let me know they had contacted that clerk.

Personally, I won't go to that donut franchise again—ever—bad service. But you know what? The Tim Hortons I go to in the morning welcomes me with open arms. In fact I know the clerk at the drive-through personally. We chat, we joke and I get excellent service...even for just buying a coffee in the morning. So make sure you are excellent at treating your customers like gold because they are.

Pinch the pennies

Finally, the other key trend to beating the recession is to look at your expenses. How many of you have had a review of all your expenses to see where you can cut back? Call your accountant and regroup...recalculate, find the waste, shop around, get deals, negotiate...just do what you have to do to stop the financial bleeding.

If you follow these five steps you will have a much better business in hand.

SELF-MANAGEMENT

We've talked about managing change and managing economic conditions and now it's time to look at how to manage *you*. In the following blog post we look at the return on investment and how managing *you* is critical for success.

MANAGING YOU

Blog Post, November 2008

I believe the most important thing to look at in your business is your R.O.I—your return on investment. I'm not using this term in the usual sense; I'm talking about the return on your investment of time, energy and money that you put into your business.

What is bringing you a good return on your investment? Is the work you're doing bringing you joy? If not, why not? Are all areas of your business bringing you a decent income? If not, why not?

Is the marketing you're doing working? I know a lot of us love to network...but really when you look at it does going to those morning networking meetings pay a dividend for you that's quantifiable?

If you're not getting a return on your investment then you might need to make some changes to what you're doing. Your R.O.I. is the payback for the time, money and energy you're investing into your business. It's the key place to look to see if the actions you're taking in your business are the *right* actions at that moment. You have to keep your eye on the goal but you may have to alter the course depending on a number of key factors such as the economy, what the market wants and needs and if the actions you're taking to market and promote yourself are the best fit for your potential customers. I liken this to a pilot who has a destination that he has to reach; however, depending on the weather patterns and winds the pilot may have to change the route or flight pattern slightly in order to take the best route to the final destination. That's the mindset you need to adopt too. You know where you want to end up but you may have to be willing to make some adjustments to your business plan along the way. But, where does it start?

Look at the return on your investments...what's working for you and what's just a bust?

Take care of you first

The next area you have to examine as you go through change and managing your business (so that it works better) is to take care of *you* first! I don't mean this in a narcissistic way but purely from the point of view that *you* matter. *Your* health, *your* wellness, *your* sanity, *your* savings, *your* money, family, social life, home, business...if they aren't firing on all cylinders then it may be time to implement some change.

When I talk here of taking care of you it doesn't mean to all of a sudden hoard your money or not be a giving, decent, loving and charitable person. It means that if you're not happy with the results in the key areas of your life then it's time to make adjustments so that those areas can now become way more satisfying to you.

If your eating habits need work then strive to develop a plan and actions that will have you making improvements. If your business needs to change, look at the areas that work and those that don't work and decide where to invest time and energy—if you even want to at all.

In some cases what might happen is you may decide to throw it all up for grabs just like a big city lawyer named Jeff Brown decided to do. He gave up his law practice to pursue a more spiritual journey. He's written a book about his experiences and his determination to bring "Unity Consciousness" to the planet. Check out the work Jeff does by logging onto http://www.soulshaping.com/. It's a powerful shift and change that speaks to his soul and life purpose.

Put a daily plan of action together and put in place some accountability to help you make changes that ensure you take care of *you* first. It could be meditation, getting a coach, being more aware of your choices and making sure that they line up with your goals.

Here is the last point about you taking care of you first...and why it's perhaps the most important. If you fly any of the major airlines you know that they always instruct you to take the oxygen mask and place it on you first even before putting it on your kids. It's not that you don't love your kids with all of your heart and might but if you faint from lack of oxygen, how on earth can you take care of your kids? So put your mask on *you* first!

Do an inventory of your life

What's really important to you? I mean really...what is it that you can't live without? Is it the big stuff? Like more technological gizmos or that new SUV? Probably not, right? I mean they're nice to have...don't get me wrong...but when you do an inventory of what's really important it's usually the simple things in life like music, reading, sipping a coffee, doing yoga, watching a sunset or walking on a nature trail.

Recognize what is important to you and put more attention and focus on that.

Make friends with being flexible

As we encounter the overwhelming amount of change that we literally face every day, we've got to really go with the flow unless we want to go crazy. What upsets us is that we think that it's supposed to look way different, right? Life has to be just so or maybe if it's not it's because we failed at it. Well I am here to tell you that whatever isn't working in your life, whatever change you're going through, it's not always a reflection of you. Sometimes it's just what is. It doesn't mean that there's anything wrong with you.

Sometimes, even with your best intentions and efforts, you may not get the ideal results you seek. So be open to change, to make modifications towards your ultimate goal and vision and have less focus on why things didn't work out for you. A good colleague once said, "You don't drive looking out your rear-view mirror so why on earth do you do that in your life?"

Focus on the what, how and when...rather than the why...and stay flexible. Don't stay stuck. The change you might be going through may not be your fault. Just move forward!

Exercise

I can't say this enough...get thee to a gym or a yoga class or a nature trail and include exercise as part of your daily to-do. My colleague Benjy Karsh, who works in sales at one of Toronto's top rated radio stations (CHUM-FM), told me something years ago that has stayed with me. He once said that going to the gym was the most important appointment he had all day.

When you exercise have some variety in your workout too so you don't get bored. Maybe have a buddy to go with so you can challenge each other and have more fun.

Surround yourself with optimistic, proactive people

Do you have a mastermind team, a coach or a mentor? If you're thinking to yourself that you don't have any of these things then you may not be getting optimum results in your business. The best of the best in business have all of these. Why? Well to quote master weight loss coach and expert Harvey Brooker from Brooker Weight Loss for Men, "If you could have done it on your own you'd have done it by now."

Sometimes you can't make change alone. Sometimes you need a *Sherpa guide* to help you climb the mountain. Put in place a mastermind team, hire a coach or, better yet, get a mentor...someone you look up to in your industry. (Review the section about team building in Section I if you need more information.)

Hold the vision

I am often reminded of Mr. Honda, the inventor of the Honda engine and motorcycle. His story is one of triumph when things are seriously challenging. He came up with his inventions amidst death and the destruction of Japan during World War II. He collected parts (gas cans dropped from planes during the U.S. bombings) to build his motor bike and he got the fuel from those empty gas cans (funny how there is enough fuel for a war...but not for people). Anyway he held his vision, despite bankruptcy, loss, and World War II, to build the Honda motorbike. Today, Honda is a leading automotive manufacturer and has led the way in building enviro-friendly Hybrids.

These times demand we be sharp and at our best. I believe that challenging times demand that we give life our very best. If we're going to have breakthroughs in life or in our socio-economic situation then we really have to be on our game right now in order to make it. We have to be in shape physically, mentally and spiritually. One way to do so is to really focus on your vision. What is it that really lights you up, turns you on and makes you giddy? Take that, bottle it and keep visualizing it happening. Isn't it a good feeling when you do?

Make a daily practice of having news fast...simply don't watch the news at night...sometimes the images and stories are deeply frightening and sad, so make a daily practice of holding onto your vision. Instead of watching the nightly news take time to meditate daily, visualize, read something positive or listen to something uplifting. The bottom line is you really need to keep your eye on your goals and what you want to happen in your life and or business. You almost have to be vigilant about it or be what I like to call a "spiritual warrior". So keep your focus. Focus daily. Feel it; let the good thoughts and visions overtake you so that they *become* you.

Take action

With respect to goals, projects, and other to-do items, it's easy to get stuck too long in the thinking and planning phase. You can sit around writing and rewriting your goals, delving into your subconscious mind, working through emotional blocks, summoning the power of Thor...whatever. But if you don't eventually get into action, you're wasting your time.

As Carl Jung said, "What you resist...persists." But if you have a challenge in front of you, whether big or small, at least take action steps to overcome it. Get educated, learn and explore the situation you need to focus your attention on and take the proper action steps needed to reach your end goal or vision. Simplify things, take baby steps and you'll get there!

Choose love

Oh gosh, I sound like a hippie now..."Choose love, man!"

Whenever you're facing change or a situation that is forcing your hand...choose love. What would love look like now? Let's say it's confrontation with someone else or it's a bit of bad news that you're facing...ask yourself..."What's the most loving act I can do for me and for the other person?" and choose that over fear or retribution.

MANAGEMENT VS. LEADERSHIP

There is a lot of talk about leading and not managing. I think that as managers and owners of our small businesses that we need to adopt this "leading" mindset. Here is why: management, or "manglement" as my good friend and fellow business coach Jamie Crookston calls it, is the tendency to mangle things that you are put in charge of running.

Why is this? My thought is that we aren't trained to be managers. So don't manage. Lead!

We can all lead. The way I see it is that when you lead you motivate others in a way that inspires them to give the best they can. If you're a solo-preneur then you lead in all areas of the business so you maximize results in every aspect of your business. For example, look at the various elements of your business. You've got accounting, marketing, finance, sales, administration, planning, community development, human resources and business operations.

What you want to do is look at each aspect of your business and see how you can maximize the results and minimize the effort. Look and see where you can save time, money and resources (both external and internal). How can you take small incremental steps to do better in each of these key result areas?

This is good leadership. You're not getting caught up in the managing of minutia but you're looking at the big picture and making improvements on a slow and steady pace in all aspects of the business. It might mean that you have to hire employees or contract out some of the work. You want to maximize your time so that it's spent on the most profitable elements of your business.

If you love making things but hate selling, hire a sales rep. If you love the marketing but need a second opinion, get a marketing coach. If you can't stand the books or the administrative paperwork, and most of us can't, then hire a bookkeeper/admin person.

When you plan each element of your business and you aim for higher heights get the help you need and stick to what you do best. Then, and only then, are you taking on a leadership role in your business.

Some experts, like international management speaker and business coach Donald Cooper, suggest you want your business to earn you up to four times what you'd earn working for someone else. It's got to make sense. It's got to make dollars too or why do it?

I love how Michael Gerber, author of the book *The E-Myth Revisited*, explains it. You want to work *on* not *in* your business. You want to develop a business that can eventually run without you. It's in this moment that as a "true" entrepreneur you can then use the extra time you have towards building another business or expanding your existing one. You don't want to just *create a job* for yourself—as Michael Gerber would suggest you want to *build a life.*

What would you have to give up in order to have total joy and passion in your business venture? What would your business look like if it was all about fun? What would need to change? What would have to happen? Who needs to do what? What work would you have to give up to get to that point?

If you can handle the things that frustrate you in your business then you're on your way to leading and not managing. Now, if you run a big business get out of the micro managing and get into the leading.

Here are some suggestions: hire people that are better at the things you're weak at and learn to trust and lose your expectations. Yes, people may disappoint you sometimes but they are, after all, only human. If you lead in a true sense of the word then you inspire people to go where you want them to go.

Look at Winston Churchill. He rallied the troops when things looked bleak during World War II. In Canada we can look to our own Prime Minister Pierre Elliot Trudeau. When asked about how he would handle and catch the FLQ (Front de libération du Québec—a terrorist group that operated in Quebec, Canada during the '60s and '70s) for the murder of Pierre Laporte and the kidnapping of Robert Cross, he replied to the media that he would do whatever it took. "Just watch me," he told them. In that moment he galvanized the nation and reintroduced the War

Measures Act…an act that hadn't been seen in Canada in 30 years.

People *believed* these men and believed *in* them; they trusted them. They felt confident in following the direction that they were taking and were on board with their policies. Sometimes leading others is not all hearts and flowers; it's about taking someone down a path less travelled. It's about taking your team over the abyss, safely.

So when it comes to management are you going to lead or micro manage? Trust me—micro managing is time consuming, energy zapping and it destroys morale. Leading does the opposite, as long as your team is on board with your vision, mission and goals.

So yes, there is more to comment on about management. But as you're starting up focus on leading…it begins with you and what you want and desire from this business venture!

MANAGE YOUR MINDSET

Sometimes the most important person to manage is you. What's between your ears? Your mindset is key to your success…some even say it's "mind over matter"…in other words, if you don't *mind,* it doesn't *matter*!

Enjoy the next post…

MANAGING YOUR FRAME OF MIND

Blog Post, December 2009

Have you ever left something you loved doing? I did just that in October. I hosted/produced my last Small Business Big Ideas

Show on CKDO on October 4. It's not because I didn't love radio or the listeners or the owners of the station, the decision to leave was borne out of necessity. With two key work commitments that took place during the week, life had been pretty full on and my body and mind needed to have a break from working six, sometimes seven, days a week.

Now it's been a month since I hosted the last show, I have to admit something to you. Come the weekends, I have been feeling flat and there is a piece to my life that's missing, leaving a big void. Those close to me could even suggest I was a little depressed especially for the first few weeks. I didn't have that something to get up for on Sunday mornings and there was no fire in the belly to do the work I really enjoyed doing. I didn't have the same mission and drive that I had when doing the show for the past seven years on Sundays.

The first Sunday off I ended up sleeping most of the day and there was a grieving process to go through. I just felt off. Perhaps it's just the body that needed to rest after going and going. Perhaps too it was the fact that once I was up on a Sunday to host the show, I would designate that day as the day to do the show, hit the gym, wash the car, do errands, clean and do laundry. Once the key part to getting up and getting going on a Sunday was out of the equation, it became easier to sleep and do nothing that first Sunday off. Plus, if you could, would you rather sleep in or get going and get excited about doing laundry, cleaning and washing the car? Yeah, you'd opt for sleeping in too...

So there you have it...I am speaking my truth. Since leaving the show, I have not had the same verve and passion to my weekends. I still feel there is a void and being slightly type "A", I need something to do. I thrive on it. In fact two weekends ago I was home in bed with a nasty cold and cough too so three out of four weeks of not doing the show were spent feeling a little blue and flat. Those that know me know I am pretty upbeat, like to laugh and have fun. But life hasn't been as fun as I'd like it lately.

Lately it's been about work, trying to make ends meet and I

have been feeling like I am on a bit of a treadmill—work, pay bills, work, pay bills. Not that I am complaining, it's just that sometimes as good as life can be it seems like you have to ask yourself if that is all there is. Now I know the process I have gone through this past month is just that...it's a process and it's part of life. This too shall pass...and truthfully to me the real heroes in life are those that are on the treadmill and don't give up. They go to work every day and make it happen. It's those of us that even though we're not at our "optimum best" don't give up—we just keep going.

It's okay to feel flat; it's okay to sleep in all day; it's okay not to be happy all the time; it's okay to be depressed now and then; and, it's okay to not be going and going all the time.

"But how so?" you ask. If we're not happy with life, how can we attract the good things we want in life? Doesn't the law of attraction state that you've got be up, positive, and happy for people to be attracted to you? I say drop it. Just be you, just be real.

Sometimes in life you're going to feel flat or a little empty. You may know intuitively that you must get back into action, get back on that court of life, but yet, something stops you. I think you have to be okay with the times when that "certain something" stops you and just take a timeout. When your little child is acting up and having a temper tantrum, what do you suggest? You've heard it haven't you? "Johnny, I think you need a timeout right now."

We also need a "timeout" as business owners. There is a time to act, there is a time to reflect, there is a time to be still and not do anything except just rest. There is a time to research, a time to sell and a time to market. The key is to stop and listen to your body. What is your body telling you? Does it need rest? What does your intuition tell you? Is it time to take a break and just be still for a while? Sometimes in the stillness you get your best ideas!

You see, in this mile-a-minute, results-are-everything world, we don't give ourselves permission to be still, to be silent and to go within. The magic of really creating something good in life is to be okay with those moments when we're not taking massive action, when we just don't have the juice left in the tank to act and create and when we need to refresh, re-energize and refuel.

We sometimes treat our own cars better than we treat ourselves. We take the car in for a check-up, we top up the fluids, change and repair things on the car…we sometimes need to take ourselves in for a check-up and regroup.

To bypass this stage is almost dangerous to your health, life and the success of your business. As I look back now at this moment where I really did feel flat, I honestly think I felt that way because on some level I was mourning the loss of doing something I loved doing. Even though I loved doing the radio show, I needed to have a break or a timeout at that time.

I had also lost my mojo—that passion to create something else…and that was okay. If you just allow those feelings to come up, eventually you will fill the void with something else, eventually you will paint your blank wall with something wonderful again, so just allow the feelings when you are feeling flat or lacking passion.

If this persists longer than three months, you may want to talk to a doctor or health care professional as it might be a deeper problem and it can border on depression. If this feeling does last longer, do talk it out and get professional help. However, if it truly is a short-term occurrence then here are some good habits to adopt when you're going through the "flat times":

1) **Talk it out.**

2) **Have a mastermind team.**

3) **Seek professional counseling.**

4) **Have a laugh.**

5) **Incorporate exercise and meditation in your day-to-day activity.**

6) **Have that one good buddy or mentor you can connect with—sometimes those close to you get tired of your stuff.**

7) **Be okay with the times when life isn't all that it can be...you have to embrace all that it is.**

But wait? You claim...this is all well and good...but life lately is really getting to me. Well, if it's of any help then know that you're not alone. Life is challenging for each one of us.

In North America we are addicted to feeling good. In a book by Barbara Ehrenreich called *Bright-Sided* the author explains how the relentless promotion of positive thinking has undermined America. Ehrenreich suggests that last year (2010) Americans spent 14 billion dollars on self-help books, CDs and seminars. Antidepressants are the most prescribed category of drugs in the country.

A review about the book in *Newsweek* magazine explored this notion that we must feel upbeat and positive all the time. Writer Julia Baird commented that according to a General Social Survey (conducted by economists Betsey Stevenson and Justin Wolfers of The Wharton School) that despite three decades of economic growth in America, men and women are no happier. This fact has been lost in the hubbub over the finding that while women were happier than men in 1972, they are not now. Barbara Ehrenreich calls positive thinking a "mass delusion". She argues that an unrelenting drive to train our brains to overlook problems and blame ourselves for failures has blinded us to inequality, incompetence, and stupidity.

Baird writes in her article, "The philosophy of positive thinking has been developed both as a reaction to the negativity of Calvinism and a salve for the sick and anxious, but has, over time, been turned into a kind of blind optimism.

At the heart of positive thinking is a belief that you can will anything you like into happening: recovering from cancer, getting a promotion, becoming a millionaire. Often, the worse things are the more vehemently people are encouraged to be sunny. The more companies downsized and restructured in the '80s and '90s, the more popular affirmation-chanting, team-building consultants became—and all the while, as the country's wealth shot up, the gap between rich and poor ballooned." (Baird, Julia. "Positively Downbeat." *Newsweek* 25 September 2009. Web, December 2009 < http://www.newsweek.com/id/216147>.)

With tragedies like Hurricane Katrina, a sagging economy, the Iraq war, and yes, even the recent H1N1 epidemic, it may not be a time for "let's get happy" but may be a time to connect to others, to team up, and to talk. It's a time for dialogue, compassion and speaking up...a time for working at making collective change to create a world we would be proud of for our grandkids. Maybe it's a time to shout out, get mad and be a little ornery. And as Baird writes, "This is why Ehrenreich dedicates her book to "complainers everywhere" inciting them to "turn up the volume". But surely there's a middle way between clueless cheerleaders and grumpy prophets. The Dalai Lama shows you can strive to be content and remain angry about injustice." (Baird, Julia. "Positively Downbeat." *Newsweek* 25 September 2009. Web, December 2009 <http://www.newsweek.com/id/216147>.)

Maybe now is the time to speak up. Drop the "happy, all is well" facade and get into collective action to bring justice, fairness and equality to all mankind. I recommend the book by Ehrenreich...and as Thomas Frank, author of *The Wrecking Crew* and *What's the Matter with Kansas*, wrote in his review of the book *Bright-Sided*, "We're always being told that looking on the bright side is good for us, but now we see that it's a great way to brush off poverty, disease, and unemployment, to rationalize an order where all the rewards go to those on top. The people who are sick or jobless—why, they just aren't thinking positively. They have no one to blame but themselves. Barbara Ehrenreich has put the menace of positive thinking under the microscope. Anyone who's ever been told to brighten up needs to read this book." (Frank, Thomas. "Bright-

Sided." Macmillan. Web, December 2009 http://us.macmillan.com/brightsided/BarbaraEhrenreich>.)

So maybe as the year draws to a close you should begin to speak up, begin to connect and make change. Join proactive groups that allow you to be a force for good. Begin to be okay with not being upbeat and happy all the time. It's okay you know.

There are lots of unbelievable, incredible people who aren't happy-go-lucky all the time and who are doing great things on the planet. Know that you're okay no matter how you feel and yes, maybe, take your *not feeling good and being upset with life*'s lot and take massive actions to make change on the planet.

So go ahead and have a *Bah, Humbug* this season. Maybe that's exactly what the doctor ordered for you to live your most powerful, authentic, real life in the future! For more information about Barbara and her books log onto her site at: http://www.barbaraehrenreich.com/.

However, if the flatness feeling continues past one or two weeks, please get professional help and call a doctor or therapist. Life is about being real, authentic and as joyful as you can be...but there are times when that's just not how you are feeling...and it's cool. Just know you should seek help when negative feelings persist for any extended period of time.

WORKSHOP

1) Who can you turn too, to help you deal with your emotions?

2) How can you manage the downs in business, are you prepared?

3) Do you have a back-up plan should your sales and successes slow down? If so what is it?

BE A WARRIOR

Now that we've had a chance for a little self-reflection, we may be ready to move ahead. It's not easy but we need to step up and be prepared to fight for what we want. Perhaps you've heard the term "spiritual warrior"? Let's look at how you can become one yourself.

BE A SPIRITUAL WARRIOR

Blog Post, June 2009

We're now into the 8th month of this "new economy" (and yes I am intentionally not using the "R" word...I won't use that word any longer) and this economy is one that's making us nervous, indecisive, afraid and unsure. So when you try these character traits on for size how does it make you feel? Not that good, huh? I agree...how can being nervous, indecisive, afraid and unsure really ever feel good?

I think it's time to turn the corner, as hard as it might be given the realities of the day and the things you hear about in the news. It's time for us to become what I call, and others have too, a "Spiritual Warrior". This can take on many meanings for us but to me when I think of a "Spiritual Warrior" I think of someone who is going to be sure in their own thoughts, who believes that good will happen, who is impervious to negativity and fights against bad news like 10 "Supermen".

I think it's time to "amp" up the positive—in our thoughts, in what we say and in what we do. You see a great deal of marketing tactics that focus on the negative or that instill fear in order to get you to change your buying habits. Although this formula works, I just am not buying into it. Tony Robbins, the master of personal growth and development, states in his book *Awaken the Giant Within* that people do things for two reasons: one is to avoid pain and the other is to have more pleasure. This "Pain and Pleasure" principle was and is used in today's marketing messages. For example, do you want to get that hot date? Well, if you have dandruff you'll never get that woman you want, but with our magic potion you can rid yourself of dandruff and have that hot date! Aw, yes, the pain and pleasure principle at work in our advertising and marketing messages.

Recently I had the pleasure of leading a training session to youth entrepreneurs and in doing so I came to the realization that when you are making a cold call and you phone someone (a prospective client) out of the blue, you've got to be super positive as to how your company is going to get that client results or how your business is going to solve your prospective client's pain. You've got to know the benefits your business venture can offer someone else and you've got to be able to communicate that to potential clients. Benefits - cost = value— that's the value equation.

If you don't know what you do for others or why your clients like you and buy from you then you better find out, and fast! In sales you've got to "amp" up the positive and show your value to each and every prospect and client you have. This means a mindset change too.

First of all you've got to believe in yourself and what it is you do. You've got to believe so strongly that you're not going to quit until you get in your client's door (unless of course the client is rude, not fun to deal with and there is just no hope at all in getting through to that client). But if there is an opening, even a slight opportunity, then you have to stick with it and nurture the client until such time that client needs what you have or has an upcoming need and wants to learn more about you and your products/services. You have to nurture that client in a positive way (don't overdo it, there is a fine line between coming on too hot and heavy and being pleasantly persistent) and stick with a client until the sale. It may mean numerous calls, contacts, discussions or meetings before prospective clients give you the opportunity to give a quote and are willing to sign the bottom line and do business with you.

If you don't believe in yourself then why will your client or prospect?

The other aspect of mindset is that you have to have drive. I say be *pleasantly persistent* with a prospective client until you get a lawyer's letter to *cease and desist* or you get physically hauled out of the building. Studies show it takes seven to nine contacts to get a deal. I believe in this kind of economy it's actually more than that; sales cycles are longer right now.

Besides drive, “amping” up the positive, and a belief in yourself, there are a few other aspects that will help you to be successful in running and selling your business. In order to become a “Spiritual Warrior” in your business venture you've also got to have patience. There is a Hindu expression I just love that talks of patience: “Have patience! In time even grass becomes milk.” That means that in time even something so impossible becomes possible—grass becomes milk. How on earth does that happen? Well, think of it for a moment. Cows graze and eat grass and eventually what they eat becomes milk. The impossible becomes possible.

Have patience...stay with it, have belief, be positive and totally sure about what you do.

What other traits do you need to be in business and have that “Spiritual Warrior” mentality? You've got to work well in teams. If you think you've got to do it all on your own...go for it...but that's the hard route. You've got to be able to lead others—to have them buy into your dream and vision for your business. Getting help in your business in the areas you need it can be liberating. Think of it this way: by getting the help you need and leading others your venture has an opportunity to grow, you free up more time for yourself, you hire others and actually help to keep the economy growing.

On the other hand, when you do things on your own you limit growth, you limit free time and you get mired in the muck (as it were) working on the aspects of the business you don't like. So a good "Spiritual Warrior" leads others as well.

Think back to how we started this article. We talked about the feelings and emotions we are experiencing in this economy—uncertainty, fear and indecisiveness. Once you begin to don your "Spiritual Warrior" mentality your feelings totally change. The new feelings include being positive, having drive, patience and looking to hire and lead others. Do you feel a difference in yourself as you take on those character traits and wear your "Spiritual Warrior" hat?

There are two other key characteristics to take on...and one of them is not to take *no* personally. Let negative results roll off of you like water off of a duck's back. Let it go. Learn from it...but let it go. You're bound to hear no from clients...especially when you're cold calling or prospecting. But you've got to be okay with the *no*. (Remember it's no *right now* and maybe not *forever*.) At least keep the lines of communication open...and play for that day when a *no* becomes *maybe* and the *maybe* becomes a *yes*!!!

The last trait a good "Spiritual Warrior" needs is to have certainty. If you think back to when Moses led the Jewish people out of Egypt after years of being slaves in that land, you know that they needed absolute certainty to part the Red Sea. Everyone had to have the same focus and thoughts in order to manifest the parting of the Red Sea. I mean how else do you pull that off? It's the power of the mind, prayer, visualization...it's about having absolute certainty that no matter how bleak things look now that in the end everything is going to work out. It means that *all* hands have to be on deck.

I remember hearing Trey Anthony, the producer and writer of the play *Da Kink in my Hair*, speak about the early days of trying to get her play launched. There were many obstacles to overcome to get the play seen and to get it to a stage. There was doubt among the cast members that the play would ever take off. Doubt kills certainty. Trey Anthony had certainty! She inspired her team to believe; they took a long-term approach and worked really hard to fill the seats. Of course they marketed like heck too!

The play went from the Fringe Festival to Mirvish Productions to Global TV. It took vision, patience, tenacity, belief, certainty, and team work—all of the characteristics of a "Spiritual Warrior".

As I conclude this posting I really encourage you to become a "Spiritual Warrior" and put these feelings and emotions to use for you.

To recap...the key traits to succeed include:

Have a strong belief in what you do for others—that what you're selling, doing or making is really about making a positive difference for someone else.

Amp up the positive. Focus on results you get for your clients and/or the good things you do for them.

Have unwavering drive.

Be patient.

Lead others to help you run your venture.

Be okay with hearing no.

Have absolute certainty!

Once you take these traits on...you'll see that it feels much better than feeling fear, uncertainty, indecisiveness and worry.

So, step up to the plate, don your "Spiritual Warrior" gear and swing for the stars this month!

HAVE PATIENCE

Practice patience. Eventually even a blade of grass becomes milk.

As business owners it's all about being in action. Action means results. But in some cases the actions you take don't always pan out. In other words you have to step back and allow things to come about. Be patient.

Some synonyms for patience include: *long-suffering, resignation and forbearance.* These nouns denote the capacity to endure hardship, difficulty, or inconvenience without complaint. *Patience* emphasizes calmness, self-control, and the willingness or ability to tolerate delay.

Some even say patience is a virtue. We study the importance of having patience in the Bible with the story of Job. Modern day psychologists refer to patience as *the art of letting go* and *acceptance.* They even go so far as to suggest coping mechanisms while you are waiting for that certain outcome. They definitely don't suggest you lose your cool and take your anger out on that person or lose your control over the situation. The gains you make for having patience far outweigh the costs for losing it!

One personal example of having to practice patience was in my efforts to arrange a radio interview with Dr. Stephen Covey. It took 14 months of phone calls (all of them long distance to the Franklin Covey headquarters in Utah), back and forth emails, tentative dates (and then not so tentative dates), go-aheads, then cancellations with numerous delays and false hopes before we finally landed the author of *The 7 Habits of Highly Effective People* for the show.

I am not too good at having patience. I like things to happen fast. My personality style is such that I like to move on things quickly...get it done, batten down the hatches and go for it. But in waiting out all those delays and false starts to getting the Stephen Covey interview my patience paid off. It's quite a coup to get a guest of his magnitude. He's one of the top minds and thinkers in business and organizational development today. He's in the same league as Jack Welch (General Electric), Ken Blanchard (Business management expert) and, dare I say, former President Bill Clinton, as far as leading speakers and modern day leaders are concerned.

Our little show on Sunday mornings on CKDO got Stephen Covey. Now I am not meaning to brag but just reaffirm that it was quite a big thing to have a guest like Dr. Covey on air with us. I didn't lose sight of my goal to give my listeners the very best there is in terms of guests and we did it. It took 14 months but we got him.

Now, what would have happened had I lost patience? What if I lost my cool? Well, you can imagine what might have happened. I would never have had the honour of speaking to Dr. Covey, my reputation would have been tarnished and I would not have been able to deliver such a guest on the show.

So the lesson is practice patience. It takes work, believe me. It takes yelling in the mirror, going for walks, working it off at the gym and dumping the anger. As you practice patience your life results will vastly improve.

Here are a few ways to be more patient and to be in the "flow" of life and just trust that opportunities will come, clients will say yes, or better yet, you too will interview a guest like Dr. Stephen Covey. I hope these tips to practicing patience will help you.

1. **Develop a consistent philosophy of life.** Take life one day at a time. Consider each day a gift of life that will allow you to get one step closer to your goal of growth and change.

2. **Break larger goals down into components that include short-term goals and objectives which are more realistically attainable in the immediate future.**

3. **Accept the reality of your humanity in that you are going to need time, effort, and energy to change and grow**. You will experience some resistance to altering long-standing habitual ways of acting, reacting, and believing.

4. **Reframe your perspective**. Live in the moment. Do not dwell on your past mistakes and failings. Begin to live each new day as a fresh start.

5. **Be systematic in planning your path to recovery and growth.**

6. **Accept, understand, and forgive yourself for being fragile, imperfect, and weak.** You need to become your own best friend and

cheerleader. Love yourself.

7. **Wake up to the realities of life around you.** Everyone with whom you come in contact is busy working through their own struggles, weaknesses, setbacks, relapses, crises, and obstacles to their personal growth and recovery. All of us are on the path to personal growth. There is no one exempt from this journey. It takes a lifetime to complete.

8. **Hand over and let go of the worries, concerns, anxieties, and doubts about attaining your goal.**
9. **Confront your fears about attaining your goal**. Remember, the world was not created in a day. Beautiful symphonies, works of art, and literary masterpieces were not created in a day. A lifetime is not lived in a day.

WORKSHOP

1) Do you feel you're a patient person?

2) How can you prevent from putting all your eggs in one basket should a project, client or sale your working on take longer than you expected?

3) Why do you feel it's important to not invest in one client, project or area of your business and have additional revenue streams to also count on?

MANAGING MONEY

Where is your money tree?

We all need money to start a business. The key is to be realistic about what you need. I just met a client who wanted to open a nightclub. When I asked about the money, he claimed he didn't have it. He was in the "dream big" mode still. So, first of all be realistic about what you need and what you can get. If you don't have access to $250,000, like this client needed, then pare down your business idea to an amount you can live with.

The other key is to live within your means. Launching a business isn't akin to a death sentence for bad behaviour; it's about creating a life and lifestyle that work.

One of my former clients wanted to start a nature tours excursion company. He researched and researched and when it came crunch time to open the business two key issues around money stopped this business idea dead in its tracks. One was that the market he was going after didn't have enough disposable income to afford to go on these tours; and second, the cost of insurance, should anything go wrong or someone get hurt, was way too cost prohibitive.

Money plays itself out in our businesses more often than not. The key is to work around the money issue and to find creative solutions to your money challenges. Start smaller, try something else that's related perhaps, shift your idea a bit, but somehow don't let money totally rain on your parade!

So when it comes to getting money be realistic, know what you need to get your business kick-started and don't overstretch yourself financially.

There are a few key places to get money. The first place, of course, is from you. You may have to tap into your own savings and resources. A good friend of mine sold his car to have money to invest into his business. He believed in it that much and years later it paid off.

The next place to look is to your family and friends. It's called "love" money. They lend it to you because they love you. But, be careful. Make sure you pay them back. You never want money coming between friends and family. It's a sure way to mess up a relationship.

Another place to look for funding is through organizations like Angel Investors and CVCA (Canada's Venture Capital Association) and in the United States the NVCA (National Venture Capital Association). Venture Capital is an option when you need big money and your business is poised for growth and results. You can't take an idea and business plan to an Angel or a V.C. without some kind of amazing track record. In other words, a good idea and a shiny business plan *don't cut it kid.* The Angels and Venture Capital folk want tangible results and a rock solid track record.

Don't forget the banks and credit unions. I like the Micro Loan Alternative too. You can borrow less money and it's not based on your credit rating. You can launch your business with a poorer credit history.

So back to the client who wanted $250,000 to open a club. What I advised him to do was to scale back and begin with a business idea for $5,000. I knew if I worked with him on developing a business plan and if he could show me a passion and love for something else that was less expensive to start, I could help him with that. It turns out his dream was bigger than his appetite, he lost interest in pursuing the dream because it was quite a daunting task and the work, the effort and perhaps even the time to fulfill this dream was a little more than he had bargained for.

You see, sometimes, you have to just start. Keep your eye on the big dream, but scale back the dream a little and just start somewhere. If you are committed to getting started here is a link to a list of Provincial Government Grants you can get if you live in Ontario: http://www.ontario.ca/en/business_program/categories/ont04_036384

If you live outside of Ontario, then contact your local government to access grants/investment dollars and tax credits. Also contact your local Board of Trade or Chamber of Commerce, they can also help you access Government Grants/Tax Credits and programs to help you realize your business dream! In the United States you'd look on www.usa.gov to help access government grants and loans. Keep in mind the old saying, "If it looks too good to be true, it probably is." You need to do your homework about obtaining grant money.

There are a couple of other places to source money from. One is from your suppliers (no one wants you to succeed more than your best suppliers). It's a win-win situation; they get your business and as you do well, they get more business. Although money might not be in the form of a loan, it might be an extended period to pay back on your invoices. You build your business by "bootstrapping" it. This term means that you build your business not on credit, but based on the business you get from your customers. You keep debts low as you grow your business from the profits you get from each sale you make. It's here that a supplier may help you out.

Factoring is another possibility. Factoring is offered by a few companies. One that comes to mind is a company called Liquid Capital. Liquid Capital has offices in Canada and in the United States. (Rick Naor is a contact person at Liquid Capital here in the Greater Toronto area.)

These companies will buy your invoices. They will collect on your invoices but pay you before the money comes in so that your cash flow remains strong. You do have to pay a service charge to get set up with a factoring company plus a percent of the invoices but when you need a quick cash injection and your cash flow is low, factoring can be a good alternative. Using factoring is an alternative way to get financing that not many business owners know about. As always when it comes to money issues you must read the fine print and do your homework. You need to set things up in advance of the time that you actually need to use factoring as an option so that when you do require that kind of financing it will already be in place and you won't be desperate and having to wait.

I mention too, only to be humourous, that if you have a rich uncle he can be a good source for capital. But not all of us have a rich uncle; however (a little editorial licensing here) if you have one, send him my way!

Again in review, here are the key places to get money:

1) Yourself
2) Friends and family

3) Banks
4) Credit Unions
5) Micro credit sources
6) Your suppliers
7) Venture Capital and Angel Investors
8) Factoring, using your client invoices
9) A rich uncle

MONEY MATTERS

I interviewed my friend and accountant, Bob Conway. I asked him about some key things you would need to think about when it comes to using an accountant to set up your financial systems. Here is the transcript of the interview. I think it will help you further prepare your business from a financial perspective!

> **Bob, what are five key areas you need to know about before you even consider launching your own business?**
>
> You want to review your research to ensure you have a clear vision of the business and go back over your market research to confirm you understand the five "P"s: Product, Price, Promotion, People and Physical distribution.
>
> Conduct any additional research to establish firm product or service requirements and build a pricing model to establish profitability.
>
> Build working paper cash flow projections by month.
>
> Test all your assumptions made in the sales and marketing sections.

Create a final Cash Flow, Pro Forma Income Statement and Balance Sheet for the first year of operation. Review each and write narratives to explain the statements.

Bob, you're a big believer of research and testing I notice!

David, if you don't test and research the market place you can lose it all. You want to go into business with eyes wide open. Usually the key source of upset in a business is when it doesn't meet your expectations.

Let me ask you a few more financially related questions, Bob. Once you're established in your venture what are five key financial considerations?

What funding do you have immediately available? How much funding can you raise easily? How much funding do you need? How long can you last without invoices being paid? Can you work on credit with suppliers?

You should have your financial house in order; it should look like a neat and tidy bedroom your Mom would be proud of.

You know who owes you money, who you owe money, your bank account is reconciled and all billing is up to date. It goes without saying that everything is current and is being followed up at regular intervals.

Proper records should be maintained at all times. If you don't keep your records up to date you cannot respond with any degree of certainty when talking to clients or suppliers. This is very important in collections because the last thing you ever want to do is try collecting from a key client when they don't owe you anything. It's just bad office practice.

Cash flow is king, isn't it Bob? Making sure that there is enough money on hand is essential to success in business and you want to clean up any messes of course, like your bedroom analogy. Okay, I have a few more questions.

Fire away David...

So we know that being your own boss can be stressful. Sometimes it's a long and lonely road we take. What are the financial benefits of launching your own business, Bob? There has to be some reason to take the risk, doesn't there?

David the obvious answer is the income tax benefits you can take advantage of and they are: deduction for home office expenses, business use of automobile, office equipment and supplies, business entertainment and memberships, dues and subscriptions. These can be quite substantial depending on the business and the revenues.

Ok Bob, I like tax savings—more for me, less for the government. Oh, and I am getting good now at mishandling my money, just like the government these days.

Tell me something else Bob...is a bookkeeper necessary right away?

There is a saying in the business world, DO WHAT YOU DO WELL AND HIRE OTHER SPECIALISTS TO DO EVERYTHING ELSE. This is so true. If you have time in your schedule to do the bookkeeping then do it, especially if you are capable, but I never recommend people take a course to learn bookkeeping. I always recommend sales courses but never bookkeeping unless it's for an employee who is doing the bookkeeping function. I suggest always getting help to get organized in the beginning, if you can't afford a bookkeeper.

Ok, so if you have a bookkeeper, why do you need an accountant?

Not every business needs an accountant. The need for an accountant is based on the complexity of the business. Many small businesses have a bookkeeper who handles all their requirements. An accountant is frequently brought in when problems arise with the CRA or when financial statements are required for outside financing. Accountants in general are much more knowledgeable about income tax matters than bookkeepers. Accountants also have greater experience and are often brought in as business advisors. Generally speaking most corporation income tax returns are completed by accountants.

What do we want from an accountant? What should we look for in a good accountant and what services should we expect?

All accountants can provide income tax and bookkeeping services although some specialize in various special areas such as international tax, business consulting, amalgamations, and litigation tax. In every case you should expect to be greeted by a professional. That's what accountants are. A good accountant will listen to your issues and let you know their opinion. Remember we are self-employed professionals so if cost is an issue be sure to ask about billing in advance.

What are the differences between a CMA, CGA and CA?

They are all Canadian recognized professional accountants. The main difference is that all CAs have passed their public accountants exams and can therefore conduct audits and review engagements. Traditionally CMAs worked in industry, specializing in cost accounting, and CGAs worked in business.

What does it typically cost to have an accountant?

The answer is dependent on the work involved and the experience of the accountant. A simple tax return for a sole proprietorship would be in the order of $500.00 whereas a corporate return would be $1,500.00. The cost to keep an accountant on retainer usually starts at $150.00.

Why do we want to think about having a board of directors?

A board of directors is not required for a small business; however, it is wise to have a number of individuals on whom you can call to discuss business. Setting up a full board of directors for a corporation is an expensive proposition as you will need to obtain errors and omissions insurance which is costly and then pay directors fees. It is usually less complicated to keep it to a friendly advisor luncheon.

The purpose of a board of directors is to have a group of advisors who approve the actions of the company.

Wow, Bob, you're a huge source of knowledge today, thanks for this. Another question, people get freaked out when doing cash flows for a new business. Why?

Well there is no hard data to go on. You're making up the numbers—sales and even expenses are based on assumptions, not actual hard data.

Bob...what are five key financial reporting documents to be included in a business plan.

You need the following in your business plan, especially if you're going for financing:

1) Projected cash flow by month for at least the first two years of operation.
2) Pro forma income statement for the years 1 and 2.
3) Pro forma balance sheet at the end of years 1 and 2.
4) Projected sales analysis by product line by month for first two years.

5) Breakeven analysis.

I hate doing my books every month; it's why I have you as my accountant. What are five key financial reporting documents each month that we need to have access to in order to make good money decisions, Bob?

David, you want to keep on track each month—know what's going out and what's coming in...

1) Bank reconciliation
2) Time analysis of accounts receivable and payable
3) Cash flow budget to actual analysis
4) Income statement
5) Sales analysis ABC list

Bob, you talked about tax and expenses before...so what can be claimed as expenses for tax purposes?

Generally these can be considered

- Home office expenses
- Business use of automobile
- Office equipment and supplies
- Memberships, dues and subscriptions
- Legal and accounting fees
- Rent and utilities
- Business travel and entertainment

So is this why having a business is often referred to as a tax shelter?

This is a misnomer but does relate to starting a business and having a loss which reduces income from other sources and therefore the income tax payable.

David, I want to conclude that you should always think twice before you spend and always think it over and talk to someone before committing to anything. Go to the bank *before* you need funds.

Thanks for this Bob. Oh, and my cheque for what I owe you is in the mail!

Ha! Likely story, but it was a pleasure answering these questions today.

PROTECTING YOUR FINANCES

Along with having the guidance of an accountant or bookkeeper, you want to be prepared from an insurance and financial planning perspective too. You don't want to go into your business without some kind of financial plan in place.

In the book *The Wealthy Barber* author David Chilton says, "Pay yourself first"—10% to you before anyone else. This is smart business thinking and good financial planning and it forces you to budget.

Co-author of the *Chicken Soup for the Soul* books Mark Victor Hansen has a book called *The Miracle of Tithing.* His suggestion is to give 10% to God or to charity when doing your financial planning. He has discovered that giving does not cause you to have less, but in fact guarantees that ultimately and inevitably you'll have more.

Some say when you have that much trust in your faith and you pay tithing (10%) you will get it back tenfold;

at the very least you will get a tax receipt when you give to charity. There are so many worthwhile causes to get behind as a business owner. In fact some businesses align themselves with a charity and make giving back part of their business motto.

America's family financial expert Ellie Kay, who has been a wonderful guest on my show and so many other TV shows in the United States, also agrees with this notion of tithing. Ellie is someone who teaches you to really save and make do with what you have so for her to suggest you give 10% to your church or to charity says volumes about how important she feels it is to give part of what you have away to those that need it more.

It's called trust, belief and knowing that what you put out for good things will come back tenfold.

For more perspective on money and investing I had a one-on-one chat with my own financial planner, Kevin Murdock at Investors Group, and asked him a few targeted financial questions. These are things that you should really be thinking about when launching or growing your venture.

Kevin Murdock is a Division Director with Investors Group Financial Services Inc.

> **Kevin, a business owner wants to accomplish a few key things while in business...the most important in my estimation is protecting one`s life style. What kind of protection plan does someone want when it comes to financial planning?**

Protecting one's lifestyle, obviously, varies from person to person or lifestyle to lifestyle. When we think about protecting "lifestyle" as individuals, we each need to define what that is, specifically, and which parts can be protected. Tangible vs. intangible if you will. It's easy to protect one's sailboat (asset) but how does one protect the desire to sail (intangible)?

When considering "tangible" vs. "intangible" items to be protected, another way to look at it is as assets. What assets need to be protected that will ensure the continuation of one's lifestyle? Further, as a small business owner, we must also consider the protection of business assets as well as personal.

And, when it comes to protection; protection from what—loss, damage, theft, value? All these things have to be considered.

When it comes to protecting assets, a very common approach is insurance. That being said, there are a number of insurance products on the market today which are quite effective in protecting both business and personal assets.

The benefit of working with an advisor is the advisor will work with the individual to identify, valuate and determine one's assets, both personal and business, and how to protect them best. The beauty of a proper financial plan is that it's tailored to the individual. There's no more of a "cookie cutter" plan for individuals than there is for a business owner. In either case, personal or business, there's no such thing as "One Plan Fits All". You need to meet with a professional, identify and determine your needs and protect them with the appropriate product.

Another key aspect in insuring the business owner is having insurance for your business partners should you go into a business partnership. What are some typical insurance plans for those going into partnerships?

When considering a business partnership many people consider things such as "Do I like the person?" "Do they know the business?" "Can I trust them?"... that sort of thing. While these are all necessary questions, unfortunately, many partners fail to ask one of the most prudent questions of them all. "Who do I want to select my next partner?" or, "Do I want my partner's spouse to be my next partner?"

Failure to identify the means by which your next partner will be identified can destroy a business. For example, John and Bill have a partnership but didn't bother to establish what would happen to their respective half of the business should something happen (death, disability) that would prevent one from working. Further to this example, let's assume Bill has a car accident and passes away. What happens to Bill's half of the business? Well, depending on the type of business or the partnership arrangement, one possible outcome could be that Bill's wife would inherit the business. If that happens, Bill's wife could decide to keep it for herself and begin working there. Or, in perhaps a worst case scenario, Bill's widow could sell "her" half of the business to anyone she wants. She may not need John's approval to whom she chooses to sell the business. In this situation, John may be helpless in preventing the new partner from entering the business.

A very simple solution to this situation would have been for Bill and John to purchase an insurance policy as a "Buy/Sell" agreement. In its simplest form, the "Buy/Sell" agreement either establishes a preset dollar value for each half of the business or a calculation which will determine the value at the time of death. If a preset dollar value was used in creating the agreement, upon the death of a partner the option to purchase the deceased's half of the partnership would fall to the other partner rather than a family member or heir.

What if you're not in a partnership but one of your employees or perhaps a business associate that you've gone in on a joint venture with is essential to the success of your business...is "key man" insurance something to look at in this case Kevin?

Absolutely! "Key Man" insurance is very popular and useful in this type of situation. If a small business has one or two people who generate a large percentage of the business revenue, it would make sense to insure this "key" person in the event they're unable to work. The idea is that should something prevent the "key" person from working the revenue they typically generate is provided through an insurance policy. This intent is to allow the business to survive while a suitable replacement is found, hopefully someone skilled enough to generate the same amount of revenue for the business.

Other than protecting your lifestyle and business, you want to plan for the future and I know you're big on succession planning. What are some aspects of having a succession plan in place that we need to know about Kevin?

Many small business owners fail to create a "personal" savings plan because they figure the business is their personal savings plan. When deciding on what type of business you want to own, one key point to always keep in mind is when it's time to retire, will the sale of your business provide you with the money necessary to enjoy your retirement. For example, if your business is a sole proprietorship with no employees, will the sale of this business generate sufficient funds upon which to retire? If not, it's imperative that the business owner create and contribute to a personal savings plan during his/her business life. If not, a business owner may find himself in business at age 80, when the original plan was to retire at age 55.

My last question to you is about creating wealth. If you read books like *Rich Dad Poor Dad* they say that one of the ways to create wealth is to be a business owner, but creating wealth via your business is essential. What does a good overall wealth

creation financial plan look like Kevin? What are some of the key elements we need to put in place so we can *work on* and not *in* our businesses?

Whether you're a business owner or an employee the elements of a strong financial plan do not change. While there are a number of ideas out there of what constitutes a strong financial plan, I prefer to keep it simple and suggest the inclusion of the following six areas:

1) Tax Planning
2) Investment Planning
3) Insurance Planning
4) Retirement Planning
5) Estate Planning
6) Cash Management

Thanks for your time, Kevin.
(Disclaimer- Insurance products and services distributed through I.G. Insurance Services Inc. Insurance license sponsored by The Great-West Life Assurance Company.)

While Kevin is *my* financial planner, *you* have to work with someone you like and trust. There is no lack of choice when it comes to hiring a financial advisor. My recommendation is that you meet with a few advisors and become more learned about your financial situation, your goals and needs. Really make sure that no matter whom you choose to help you plan financially that you have found someone that's best suited to your needs. You have to play with the cards you're given and do your best but don't have your head in the sand when it comes to money. Make money work for you.

Just know you do need a plan and even if you can save *just a little* each month that's a beginning. And it may be better from a tax point of view, for example, to tuck some money away in an RRSP or Tax Free Savings Account—talk to your advisor.

Get a financial planner, have a financial plan in place, have insurance in place, save money for that rainy day, have a tax strategy and have a retirement plan and an exit plan as well. At the end of the day you'll know you've got things covered and it'll be one less thing to worry about.

I also recommend reading books about money too. Ellie Kay has several really practical books and David Chilton's *The Wealthy Barber* is a classic and now he's just released *The Wealthy Barber Returns*. Study about money, plan and be prepared. You know I was at a financial seminar a number of years ago and the speaker said that we spend more time planning for a vacation than we do our financial situation. Be a student, be smart with your money, learn from others who have chopped debt and are saving.

I don't think there is a magic pill here to being smart with money. Maybe my mom had it right after all when she said that you've got to "cut your coat to suit your cloth".

Get your finances in order as you move into the world of self-employment. It's vital to your success and peace of mind too. Also have a back-up plan in case your business doesn't work out as hoped. I like what David Chilton advises in his new book *The Wealthy Barber Returns*—just say this phrase a little more often, "I can't afford it right now." It doesn't mean you won't be able to afford it one day, just not right now!

To close, you may in fact need to get a part-time job not related to your business. A part-time job is a good thing to have so you've got cash flow coming in and can build your business up while still earning a steady income. Believe me, a $1000 a month part-time job usually pays the mortgage or rent at least. Yes, you might have to work somewhere for 10-15 hours a week, but it allows you time to build your venture up without as much pressure.

I am not a fan of being under pressure to sell and succeed in your business; it should be more effortless...and come easily.

We're going to delve into another good management practice and that's to get a money team around you to help you succeed and stay on track. It's easy to waste time these days and get distracted from what's really important in your business. Having that support in place keeps you focused and accountable!

MANAGING BUSINESS OPERATIONS

This is the part of the business that's often the most challenging. In a business plan, *operations* deals with how your business runs. I challenge you to take a holistic view of your business and break it down into these sections: sales, marketing, accounting/money management, production, human resources and customer service.

Under each aspect of your business you want to write a recipe of how you plan on running or executing each key component. For sales, it's how you sell—from how you find a client, to the processes you go through to turn a prospect into a paying customer. You want to list the steps or the methodology that you go through from start to completion.

It's the same for how you handle the accounting and money management of your business. How long does it take to invoice a client? How do you handle late paying clients? How do you send an invoice—is it by mail or email? Do you include a thank you note? What are the steps you take to handle the money and accounting aspect of your business? Write them down and this then becomes your operations manual.

You want to make running your business easy for you or anyone else to follow. "So," as Michael Gerber, author of the book *The E-Myth Revisited* suggests, "that you're *working on* and not *in* your business." What this means is that when you work on designing your operations manual or your "recipe" book for how your business is executed and delivered from beginning to end, you want to have the goal in mind that one day someone else can handle the day-to-day operations of your business. At this point you can back off and get into the management of it all—the planning and the strategizing.

Show of hands (again, figuratively speaking) how many of you reading right now knew you had to write an operations manual? Not many of you...just what I thought.

If you want to grow your business (and not be chasing your tail doing every task and burning yourself out) you will begin designing a business that doesn't totally depend on you being there.

Here is a question to ask yourself: Could your business survive if you were away on holiday for two weeks? If you answered no then you need to revisit your business so that it can run without you and still make money.

One of the key challenges small business owners have is giving up part of the control of the business. One way to handle this is to give up some of the control and ease your employees into more and more responsibility as they become ready for it. So if you need a marketing person, have them start out just making calls. Once they have mastered that move them onto doing marketing mailings. When they have a handle on that then move them onto managing your online social marketing plans. After a while you have a well rounded marketing person that can handle numerous tasks.

Remember a good employee isn't built in a day!

As far as where you need to focus your time in your business, I believe you've got to put most of your emphasis on sales and marketing, especially in the beginning. Your chief aim is to get clients. As you start a venture, you've got to put your time, talents and energy into attracting clients. You've then got to retain them, keep them happy and service them.

In some cases as time goes on, you have to spend time **reactivating** lost clients. Reactivation means you ask clients to come back and do business with you. In reality, you will lose clients and sometimes it's not your fault. Perhaps they have just fallen in love with another vendor because you just didn't pay enough attention to them.

Reactivation strategies include having a meeting, sharing an offer or discount, or just doing something special to get that client back. Look at your attraction, your retention and your reactivation strategies and see what you've got to do in each circumstance.

So there you have it. Your operations manual is a recipe book as it were of *how* you do *what* you do in every aspect of running your business. Take time creating one—break it down and keep your focus on the "big" three: sales, marketing and managing the money. It's in these sectors that a company tends to fail or succeed big.

Make sure too that if your sales skyrocket that you will be in a position to handle the increased production demands and the greater financial risk and paperwork involved in having increased receivables too.

View your business holistically...it's bigger than you at times. The faster you can focus on the aspects of the business you love to work on, the faster you can hire someone to help you with the things you don't and the better off you will be and the faster your business will grow.

Good luck.

BUSINESS PLANS

I realize I have written a business book without really addressing doing a business plan.

You need a plan or you can plan on failing.

I have seen terror overcome some business owners when it comes to writing a business plan.

I urge you not to fret.

Your business plan ideally is your road map, it's the story about you, your business, the market, the financial issues, the how you're going to take it from idea to market and it will also include who you're going to hire, what you're going to do, what your goals are, why you're doing what you're doing and when are you going to do what you say you're going to do.

Marketing

So let's examine the marketing section of your business plan. You have to include a complete analysis of the market you want to work with. Why them? What do you know about them? Do they need your products and services and are they already using them?

You want to know who your competitors are. Why are they strong? What aren't they doing that you can hone in on?

What are your competitors Strengths, Weaknesses, Opportunities and Threats as it compares back to your business?

A lot of companies start because the competition is missing something - there is a gap in the marketplace that is not being served.

But before you move in on that gap, ask yourself and find out why hasn't someone else done this? The reason may be it's just not that good an idea!

You want to always have your pulse on the market, whether it is for your business plan or just for you to be able to gain a competitive edge.

In your marketing section you need to show your knowledge of the customer, the marketplace, the competitor and how you're going to reach that market.

How will you advertise? Why will you advertise? What will you spend and allocate for marketing and advertising costs?

Operations

This is a key section that focuses on the how you're going to do what you're going to do. The key of any business is to make money. Whether you're a not-for-profit, a corporate business or a social purpose enterprise you need to know how you're going to make money and get customers.

Everything you do in your business is about that.

I like the R words when it comes to discussing your operations:

One is your operations basically become the "**Recipe**" for how you do and run your business.

The other R word is how do you "**Reach**" your prospects? What methods of advertising, promotion and networking are going to "Reach" your prospect.

How can you get them to "**React**" to you marketing message? What will you say that will get the attention of your customers? You might need a good copy writer to help you craft your business story or message. But a good place to look for a message that is going to get people to "React" is one that talks your customers language.

Does your message show benefits for your customer, does it show you understand their problems and you've got a solution for them? Does it showcase your successes with other clients? What will you say that will get your customer to "React"?

Once the customer reacts, how will you "**Respond**"? How do you greet them as they come into your store or call you?

What are the selling steps you take a client through? Do you seek to understand their wants and needs or do you go for the sale without knowing your customer?

How else do you respond? Is there follow up after a sale? Do you guarantee your work? Are you there before, during and after the sale?

The next R word you need to consider as it pertains to your operations is how do you show "**Reliability**"? Do you continue to work on the client relationships after the sale?

I went to buy tires about 8 years ago...and the tire store sold me tires but let me go once I paid for them without asking to get my contact information. They let me go.

If they took time to get my information and asked me if I wanted to be on their email list or be notified of deals and specials, they would have had me for life. In fact, about 6 months after you buy tires, you need an alignment or balancing. That tire store could have called me to bring me back in every so often to ensure the safety of my car and tires and they would have had repeat business and sales in between the time I bought new tires and the next time I needed to change them.

I figure that tire store lost an extra $400-500 from me, by not staying in touch.

The next R word in your operations is to focus on how you can get "**Repeat**" business. For gosh sakes, reach out, call your customers once in a while. They don't bite and they might spend more if they're feeling the "Love" from you!

Repeat business is about retaining too. How will you retain a customer?

There are so many new ways too. I mean we have online social media to use, we have mobile websites, mobile apps...there are so many ways to stay in touch so that you can retain your customers and get "Repeat" business.

Lastly the other R word you have to think about in your operations is how you might "**Reactivate**" a client gone wrong. Sometimes, people switch. Sometimes for good reason and sometimes it's just based on a feeling and emotion in the moment.

Yes...I love going to my barber, but sometimes, I go elsewhere. I go elsewhere, not because I don't like my barber, but because, I may need a haircut and for convenience go to a shop I am nearer too in that moment. You have to work on reactivating your clients that leave you so they can come back.

After all these "R" words comes "S"...how you do what you do to get a customer to come in, come back and stay with you, you have to teach to your "**Staff**" and get them to be able to be empowered to treat your customers right.

A "T" word is next...and you always have to **teach** best practices in all aspects of the business. Study other business models, learn from others and adapt the best practices of others into your operations.

Financials

Your business plan should show an understanding of what it's going to cost to get into business, how much you will need from a bank, how much you will invest into it, what risk level you can live with, how much you think the business will make in the first one to two years and what ongoing monthly costs will be.

Once you answer all of these, you will get a good picture of whether or not this business is worth it. Can you do it? Can you afford it? Do you need to scale back? All of these questions will and should be answered when you research how much it will cost you to get into business.

Risk

You have to get clear on the risks of being in business. There are financial risks, environmental risks and market risks. What is your financial risk tolerance? How much debt can you live with? What do you need to live on? Do you have money tucked away in case of a rainy day?

Environmental risks are the kinds of risks such as a new government policy that has been introduced. For example, years ago I sold promotional products. One of the biggest users of logoed pens, bags, t-shirts etc, were pharmaceutical companies.

They ordered a lot of stuff to give to doctors to promote their brands. Well, the government of Canada stepped in back in the late 80's and said, "NO"! No more incenting doctors to choose your brand, the government basically told Big Pharmaceutical companies that you cannot give stuff away.

So that environmental change affected sales in the promotional product business at that time.

A market risk involves changes to the marketplace, your clients and staff that affect your business negatively. What if your best clients files for bankruptcy and cannot pay you?

What if your employees come in late or are rude to a customer?

You have to manage risk in business...be aware and have a plan to do so!

Personnel

Who are you going to hire? What positions do you need filled? What are you looking for in an employee? These are questions you have to know about. When it comes to hiring you have to know how to conduct an interview, what questions you can and cannot legally ask.

How do you structure a want-ad?

How do you teach your team?

What are your expectations of your team?

What do you offer them to keep them motivated and enthused?

Who do you want on your team? Where do you need help the most?

Can you contract out or do you really need to hire?

I recommend you talk to an HR professional to get up to speed on the best practices when it comes to hiring and engaging employees.

Nothing can cause more grief, time and money when you make a bad hire or you're not a good boss to work with.

Really set boundaries with your team, have a supportive environment, empower and teach your people...but know that no matter how hard you try to be a progressive company and boss, people come and go...and so it goes!

In Canada you can contact the government (federal) for information on the Human Resources aspect of your business by logging onto http://www.hrsdc.gc.ca and in the United States get in touch with the government there too, because hiring, retaining and motivating employees is definitely an art!

Get in touch with the department of labor in the United States to get clear on employment laws, do's and don'ts by logging onto www.doleta.gov.

As you soldier on with your business plan, I need to share some good news...there is a new concept in the small business world called a "One Page Business Plan." According to some experts this is all you need now if you're doing your plan for just you.

Gone are the days of doing a 50 page business plan...you can achieve in one page (okay maybe 5 pages) what used to take a 50 page plan.

Other elements you need to include in your business plan are how you're going to sell and to whom.

Sales Plan

You need to know how you're going to sell and to whom. What sales channels might work? Are you a direct seller? Or a re-seller, a wholesaler, an MLM company, a distributor, manufacturer?

Did you know that GM (General Motors) doesn't sell cars to the consumer? They sell to their dealers and the dealers sell to the consumer.

Companies like Isagenix, Amway, Pre-paid Legal Care are examples of Multi Level Marketing sales. Where the more people you have buying and selling the product under you, the more you earn!

My local computer guy is a re-seller of Microsoft software, he has the rights to buy and re-sell it to his clients.

You need to get clear of the model that will work for you.

Are you business-to-business or business-to-consumer? There is a difference in how you sell if you're selling to companies versus selling to a consumer. Get familiar with those differences, find out who is doing well at it and follow their lead!

What is the process of how you will sell? We talked about that already but you need to know how you will attract, approach, connect, sell to and follow up with your customers.

You also need to know how much money you want to sell What do you want to go for? What's your goal?

The last piece to consider when writing your marketing plan is the Executive Summary...

Executive Summary

This is the section that sums up why you're in business, who you are, what you bring to the table, who your customer is, how much you need, how much you will make and what your plans are. It's a summary of your business...it is the who, what, where, when, why and how of your business plan.

It should tell the story of why you are in business, what you're doing and for whom?

Plus you might include your vision and mission statement and an elevator pitch.

You will need your plan for you first, if you are intending to go for financing the bank or the lending organization will want to see it.

They want to know the reason you're in business, is there a market, how you will capture that market, how much money you will need from them and if you can pay it back. See, there is always a hitch when it comes to getting financing, somewhere in the fine print the lender always wants it back.

If you need more information on writing a plan go to www.bplans.com or look up an Google the One Page Business Plan idea, I really like that, because I am all about ease as I get older.

You can also go to your local library, Chamber or Board of Trade or the local economic development office as they have samples of plans and show how you can write them too and lastly your bank manager can help you write your plan, many banks and credit unions in Canada have software online that helps you write a business plan.

BUILD YOUR OWN BUSINESS OR PURCHASE A FRANCHISE?

This is always a bit of a dilemma for a lot of people looking to start a new business. Franchising is a very viable idea and way to start your own business. You're buying a successful business model and working it. Usually, the franchise helps you with finding a location, marketing, consulting, buying and even building the location. With a franchise you don't need to reinvent the wheel. You've bought a business in a box as it were, but there are a number of things you need to think about before you take the plunge and buy yourself a McDonald's...

I spoke with Gerri Sefi this past August (2011) about this topic. Gerri is a business coach with Entrepreneurs Source. Entrepreneurs Source is an international company that helps "would-be" franchise owners make the right buying decision.

Here is our interview:

Gerri, why consider buying a franchise?

Franchising is often referred to as a turnkey operation, or cookie cutter methodology. When starting one's own business, cost is important but should not be the only factor to consider. One of the most important challenges will be to minimize the time frame for the business to ramp up, start producing the product or services, attract clients and, of course, commence cash flow.

The franchisor has:

a. Completed and tested the blueprint for the business.
b. A wealth of experience in what has, and what has not, worked. It has already tried, tested, accepted or rejected every aspect of the business.
c. Current information on demographics, competition, market strategies and emerging markets.
d. Made a commitment to profitability and partners with franchisees to increase revenues. Their future is your future i.e. win-win.

Rather than have to go through creation, labour and delivery of the product/service, the franchisee's focus is to learn the system, build the business plan and implement it—all of which is conducted under the guidance and watchful eye of the development team.

I think we need to know why we should consider buying a franchise over creating a business for ourselves. What are the benefits to buying a franchise?

a. Proven Method–first and foremost it's a proven method: the franchisor has already developed a model that has been successful for others. Guesswork is eliminated and risk is minimized.

b. Name Recognition–consumers prefer familiarity and consistency. For example, when you last stopped for a coffee in a strange town and ordered a coffee at Tim Hortons the beverage would have been exactly the same as your local brew. The only difference may be cost as that is local market driven.
c. Strength in Numbers–you are in business FOR yourself, not BY yourself, by having a network of non-competing other franchisees, you can exchange marketing ideas and receive quick feedback to resolve challenges.
d. Improved Buying Power–simple economics–the more you buy, the cheaper the price. Having multiple franchisees buying the same goods will significantly reduce the price.
e. Access to Capital–it is possible you will need start-up capital. Many franchisors have a financing program already in place for qualified applicants. Or, they have financing arrangements with lenders based on the strength of their brand.

How much money do you need to buy a franchise on average?

There are three important numbers to consider:

a. The Franchise Fee–this is a one-time payment to the franchisor when the agreement is signed and covers the license to distribute the product or service, training and support.

b. Business Expenses–this is the amount of cash needed to start the business, e.g. equipment, lease costs, vehicles, etc.
c. Personal Expenses–this is the amount of cash needed to live while the business ramps up. It is generally recommended that the franchisee have three months' living expenses available.

It's impossible to give an "average" number because of the wide range of franchises available today in so many differing industries–from coffee to pet grooming to home inspections. The investment can range from $30,000 to $5M for a chain of motels.

The total cost of starting the franchise will also vary as it will depend on the product or service and if the business has to lease space or can be run from a home office.

How long does it take to be profitable?

This is also a huge variable and will depend on the franchisor, product/service, model and location. Regulations do not allow the franchisor to guarantee earnings or the time it will take to become profitable. The reason for this is that they cannot know how YOU will actually run the business. However, many franchise companies declare earnings and profit of existing franchisees in their Disclosure Document—this is called Item 19 and they are only allowed to produce this under strict regulatory guidelines. Although this is not a guarantee, it can be seen as an indicator of what profit the business could be capable of achieving.

What should you look for when buying a franchise?

The product/service—does it interest you? Although the business is a vehicle for your lifestyle, it's still important to enjoy the work and have fun.

Where is the franchisor in its life-cycle? Is it a new, innovative business that has been franchising just a few years and is poised for growth? Or is it a well-established, well-oiled machine that is tried and tested? The answer will depend on both your risk tolerance, and your comfort level with new versus old.

Will the franchisor offer both initial and on-going training, and what other support do they offer?

Is the franchisor innovative i.e. do they keep abreast of economic, geographic and social changes to ensure their product remains viable and profitable?

Where are other franchisees i.e. are you alone in a new country/territory or are there experienced franchisees to learn from and lean on?

What is the expected ramp-up period i.e. how soon will the first dollar come through the door?

Is the territory guaranteed and would you have right of first refusal for adjacent territories?

Does the franchisor have an exit strategy and will they help you to sell the business?

How do you know what franchise is right for you?

Does the business meet your lifestyle dreams? If you want to work business to business, weekdays only, then even if the product excites you, retail may not work.

What business model interests you—brick and mortar, mobile, virtual and/or home based?

What are your transferable skills? Knowledge of the business is not always a requirement–the skills you bring to the business are crucial e.g. if you dislike talking to large groups of people, you may not want a business that requires you to give seminars or presentations.

Use your imagination–can you see yourself running the business? Fit is important.

Is the investment range comfortable for you, even if you have to borrow?

Do you feel that the franchisor is committed to its product and franchisees? Have you developed trust and rapport with those you will deal with on a regular basis?

What are the five biggest challenges about owning your own franchise?

A franchise is no different to an independent business, regarding life/work...it's hard work!

Now as far as challenges go, I think anyone considering a franchise needs to be aware of these...

1. The larger investment up-front instead of gradual capital injection as the business grows.
2. On-going fees—most franchises will take either a percentage of revenue, or a fixed cost as this is how the company itself makes a profit. This can be challenging in lean times.
3. Exit strategy–contracts vary of course but 10 years is fairly common. You may not be able to easily sell the business as, unlike a normal sale of a business, the franchise company will want to approve the new buyer. It's not just a question of capital, fit is important.
4. You may not agree with some of the decisions made by the management team. Rarely is a franchise company a democracy so you have to be prepared to live with what works for the majority.
5. Misconceptions from other professionals. You may hear that franchises are a "rip-off" and that only the franchisor will make money. This is patently untrue, as research proves, but it can be challenging to defend a

franchised business rather than a small independent one.

What makes a good franchise operation?

There are a number of factors that contribute to a good operation, notwithstanding the obvious i.e. that both franchisor and franchisee are profitable.

Management tenure–this is often a good example of how solid the business and staff longevity indicate that management knows how to keep good employees. Their philosophy for franchisees will often be the same.

Franchises are awarded–not bought–so it's important to assess the quality and quantity of corporate data provided to you. All companies have pros and cons and it is important that you are given as many details as possible before you make a decision.

Does the franchisor have initial and on-going training and are they accessible to assist and guide you when required?

Does the franchisor have an advisory group i.e. does management listen to those in the field, or are all decisions made unilaterally?

What is life like as a franchise owner?

Franchise owners experience much the same work life as any other small business i.e. you are responsible for everything from marketing to administration to technology. In my experience, very few small business owners ever completely leave the business behind when they leave for the day—business owners are never "off-duty". However, the franchisee has an added dimension to his business in that he has support and assistance from the franchisor, as well as access to non-competitive associates, some of whom will have been in the business longer and are experienced with the business cycle. The anxiety of having all the responsibility is somewhat mitigated by being able to share with those in exactly the same position in the same industry.

What are some of the work life expectations?

Even if you choose a business that operates during business hours, owners rarely work 9-5, no weekends. Be prepared to work harder than you have ever done before but with the knowledge that all the rewards are yours as well as pride and satisfaction.

What are the top 5-10 skills needed to own a franchise?

1. **BELIEF**—Will you trust and use the system you purchased?
2. **TRUST**—Can you follow someone else's rules? Although you may have extensive business experience, you won't yet know every facet of your new business. You will need an open mind to listen and learn about a system that has already been proven to be successful.
3. **ENTHUSIASM**—Are you willing, able and eager to learn new skills?

4. **CHANGE**—Can you set aside old habits and beliefs and embrace your new environment?
5. **STRONG WORK ETHIC**—You are no longer an employee who leaves it all behind at the end of the day knowing that someone else will ensure your pay cheque is processed correctly. Are you willing to put in the time and effort required to push and pull your business to success? Are you willing to take responsibility for every aspect of your business?

Thanks Gerri, this will be helpful for someone who is considering a franchise as a business option.

We've talked about some very key issues in this book: sales, marketing, money, investing and attitude. Some say that your attitude determines your altitude. If you're attitude is positive then you will soar in your life. Let's explore this elusive notion of success and see if we can't create a barometer to measure our own individual success by.

MODEL AFTER SUCCESSFUL BUSINESSES

I like to model my business after other successful companies and in the following blog post I take a look at some Canadian companies that are making it! We find that success leaves clues...

MANAGING FOR SUCCESS

Blog Post, July 2011

I love the June issue of *Profit,* a Canadian magazine much like *Inc.* in the United States. I love this June issue the most because it features 200 Canadian owned businesses that are succeeding. In this day and age as a small business owner we need all the good news we can get and we also need inspiration so that we can become successful in our own right. It also gives small business owners hope.

Success also leaves clues. I find it important to know what it is that's making these business owners successful and why they are growing when a lot of us are having challenges just getting a sale. Let's look a little deeper at this issue of *Profit* and see what characteristics Canada's Fastest Growing Companies share.

For starters, they aren't just doing business in Canada. Most, if not all, are taking their business to other countries. The U.S. is expected, but South America and Western Europe have been growth centres for these Fastest Growing Canadian Companies.

These business owners are taking advantage of Revenue Canada's Scientific Research and Experimental Development (SR and ED) incentive programs. Started in 1986, the SR and ED program is intended to encourage corporate investment in research and development in Canada. On average over 18,000 businesses in Canada receive over $4 billion in SR and ED tax credits and incentives annually. One more interesting fact is that nearly ¾ of the businesses that apply for these government tax credits are small business owners.

Grant money can help your venture too. If you're producing a music CD, Factor is a government grant that can help you launch and produce it. Trillium is there for arts and cultural grants and you can log onto MERX, a website that lets you bid on government tenders and programs.

So, two things are leading to success: one is doing business abroad and the other is to source government funding, tax credits and/or manufacturing credits along the way.

One other key to the success of this year's Top 200 Fastest Growing Canadian Companies is that they are open and transparent with their employees. They share the books and let those that work for them know the bottom line.

I am reminded of a good business associate of mine who owns some high-end, leading clothing stores in the United States. After the recession really hit three years ago their sales went down. So much so that they would have had to cut back the very staff that had made that retailer a top-notch success. So, what did they do? How did they handle the downturn with their employees?

Well, they told the truth and then asked them to take a temporary pay cut instead of having to lay people off. Surprisingly, the staff agreed and once the economy settled and sales picked up a bit, so did salaries. A big disaster was averted and no one lost their jobs.

One other key to success for Canada's Fastest Growing Companies is that they really invest in their people from a training and development perspective.

Writer Rick Spence states in this issue of *Profit*, "Talent is scarce—and will become more so as the job market recovers further. So, growing companies must find the right formula for keeping their most effective employees happy. Increasingly, PROFIT 200 firms are investing substantially in their employees' professional development. By offering various forms of skills training, they're keeping their top talent challenged, engaged—and around."

Spence goes on to share how Winnipeg's Broadview Technologies is succeeding at employee engagement and excellence. Spence adds, "President Michael Orloff says the company's growth (267% over the past five years) stems from seven core values that guide Broadview and its people: sustainability, unity, service excellence, strategic advice, accountability, balance and mastery. The last of these is key because the tech world changes so fast that employees who don't continually expand their skills will leave their clients underserved or at risk.

That's why Broadview has adopted a training program, or road map, for every one of its 20 employees."

Another key success trait includes building resiliency. In this day and age of such massive change, it's important to be adaptable, creative and to be able to shift thinking.

Barry Jinks of Spectrum Signal Processing Inc. (telecommunications) turned his company around by adopting a flexible mindset. According to Jinks, he was going to build new technology on profit, not via the Venture Capital route. Jinks shares his secret for success as being able to embrace new options, being open to listen to the opinions of others in the industry and willing to take massive action. Terms like innovation, drastic action, nimble, listens, seek new ideas and advice are all key to having a fast growing company in Canada today.

One other key trait to having a successful business in Canada is to think big and build on it. According to Rick Spence, "As your company grows bigger and more complex you'll need standardized formulas for keeping up with your business' and employees' performance. The earlier you start implementing proper business processes and systems, the better you'll stay in touch and out of trouble.

When asked about the systems that make his company run, Kevin Higgins pulls out a thick binder marked '2011: Better, Stronger, Fitter' from a stubby bookshelf in his exposed-brick Toronto office. It contains all the top-level paperwork he needs to run Fusion Learning Inc. (No. 146), a sales training company with 17 employees and $5 million in sales." (Spence, Rick. "5 Winning Strategies of High Growth Companies." *Profit* 1 June 2011. *Profit Guide*. Web, July 2011. <http://www.profitguide.com/article/28256--the-5-winning-strategies-of-high-growth-companies>.)

Developing systems is nothing new. But who's done that really well? McDonald's is based on a system and so is Tim Hortons. My local Goodlife Fitness Club has a system for how they greet a new customer and a recipe for customer service—they call it "a world-class meet and greet".

When was the last time your customer experience was world-class?

You need systems, policies and procedures for every aspect of your business, from how you answer the phone, to what your sales process is like, to how you invoice or even get a product to a customer. I suggest working on one aspect of your business each month and looking at ways you can create a system. Once systems are taught and procedures and how-tos are shared with employees, you can then let them run your venture while you handle the more engaging aspects of the business that you love to do.

I highly recommend this issue of *Profit*. I love the lessons shared and I love calling on these companies to engage and do business. I find that successful companies that are growing are an ideal customer.

YEAR END PLANNING

You've got some great ideas and you and I have learned a lot together so far—let's start to wrap things up a bit. Now you need to put a plan in place and follow it to succeed.

MAKE YOUR YEAR END COUNT WITH A LITTLE BIT OF PLANNING

Blog Post, December 2009

You know in December when you're wrapped up in the holiday spirit and perhaps a little less focused on your business? Make sure you take time to plan too and pull yourself away from the carton of eggnog to work on what it is you want to create for the following year.

I sense as business owners we don't plan enough. We don't give ourselves a timeout to plan on a regular basis, but to me there is something sweet about completing one year and preparing for a new one...with a plan and goals in mind.

I equate year end planning to the last part of a football game. We are well into the 4th quarter of the business year and just like in a football game, the 4th quarter is the last chance to make some big plays and win. As your year draws to a close, you want to make a big play too.

In football the 4th quarter is *do or die* time. You might see a big pass or a big touchdown, or great defensive stand...or the quarterback throwing a long bomb "Hail Mary" kind of pass hoping that the receiver catches it and gets a fast touchdown or a big gain in yardage.

Isn't it like that now for you in your business or life? It's time for the big play. Or do you breathe and take the loss but begin to prepare properly for the New Year ahead? I say that you are the one with the time clock...you're the only one putting pressure on you to throw that long bomb...or make that big play now!

Do an analysis of your life or business and begin to plan out what really needs tending to now! Rank the importance of the key areas of your life and if it is highly important to make change, make change now. Don't wait. Work on the major concerns first. Make the calls and take the actions needed to change what it is that's affecting you or hurting you most.

If it's money, call a financial planner and get an action plan going. If it's debt, talk to a trustee in bankruptcy and work out a plan for creditors. If it's a health issue, call the doctor, go to the gym and get a personal trainer or a nutritionist. If it's a family or relationship issue, get counselling, reach out, come to a compromise, and get some help to right the ship at home. If it's a work issue, work on your resume, start networking and talk it up with others to maybe make a job change.

If you need more accounts and clients, reach out, make an

action plan to meet 15 new clients in the next month and really make things happen: network, form a joint venture and ask for referrals...just grow your business.

The fact is you have to take action and although there is no time clock on you to get going, you do want to get going on the most important things first. Begin with your most pressing issues first—get into action, call the people and contacts you need on your side to help you take care of the things in your life that need changing the most.

So today, I encourage you to take that first step. You're in the 4th quarter and it would be nice to end every year (or game) with a touchdown!

Go team!

PART 6: FUTURE TRENDS

I think as business owners you have to watch what's going on around you. You have to study the marketplace, the social trends, the changes, the government legislation and laws. By having a learning mindset it will help you be ahead of the game, you can position your business where business and the socio-economic trends are pointing. You can be there when opportunity happens.

In a blog post I wrote at the beginning of 2010, I identify some key trends to watch for and get your business ready for as well. I hope this posting offers you some ideas for your venture...

THE TREND IS TOWARDS MAKING COMMUNITY STRONGER

Blog Post, January 2010

Was 2009 a year or what? 2009...we saw the arrival of the first ever Black President...the challenges that the economy brought, tighter money supplies, record bankruptcies, the loss of Michael Jackson and Farrah Fawcett on the same day, baseball's New York Yankees spending their way to a World Series, loss, divorce, challenges both personally and professionally and so much more.

So take a moment now to pat yourself on the back if you're still standing and in business! As small business owners we've collectively survived one of the most interesting years in history from a global economic front to changes in the environment, to changes in politics, media, communications and how we do business and live our lives.

Sadly, the change is going to continue. So brace yourselves.

Be open, go with the flow and don't get too attached to any one outcome, as long as you're well, alive and you have friends and family that love you...you're doing awesome!

On a personal note, this year has been a year of tough sledding—working hard and not having a lot to show for it from a financial point of view at the end of the year. I am opting for joy in the New Year...joy is my operative word. Yet, the hard work and tough sledding had many rewards in other ways for me this year. The spiritual rewards and the fact that I have touched a lot of lives is where my currency has come from.

Maybe, that's what the world is asking all of us for now. Maybe it's not about the material possessions or the *stuff* but about how we can affect lives (for the better) and help people be all they can be.

In my work in the non-profit field, I see newcomers to Canada with little or no hope as they arrive in a new land. I have also seen Canadian-born citizens go through job loss and change and uncertainty...it's been a tough year for everyone it seems, but what I have also seen is that somehow we've all made it through.

I am hopeful as I write this newsletter because I believe that the human spirit and kindness will rule the day. I have come to the realization even more this year than ever that we are our brother's and sister's keeper. If you think you're not...think again.

We've all been touched by some kind of life altering event this year and we have to begin to think that we exist for each other. We need to remember that family and community come first, rather than the "me" first we've seen during the '80s and '90s.

Now this isn't to say you aren't important—you totally are. You've got to manage your well-being on all levels or you won't be good to anyone. But once you've managed your life and wellness, then you have to step up to make the community stronger.

We need new ways of doing business. We need access to money from somewhere other than the bank because we can't always qualify for a loan (if for example we've fallen on tough times). Thus came about the concept of Micro loans...geared to helping those who are poorer or have had credit issues. The bottom line is its new thinking. It's helping those that need the help the most.

We need communities to come together to help each other. In some communities, for example in the U.S., people are coming together and organizing community swaps. Need a new ladder but don't have the money to purchase one? Do you have a lawn mower you don't need? Well maybe you can swap it for that ladder at a Community Swap. Do a Google search on Community Swaps and you will see that it's fast becoming a growing trend.

Three more examples of communities coming together include something called **transitional communities, Slow Money** and **community micro loans for businesses.**

On a CBC radio documentary that aired in September 2009 on Sunday Edition, writer David Gutnick commented that Slow Money was born out of what's happened in business and society this past year. Gutnick suggests, "Combine poisonous factory-farm tomatoes with disgraced investment banker Bernard Madoff. Then throw in a stock market disaster that cost investors their life savings. You may have the recipe for a revolution: a public spooked by the dangers of industrial food production and investors wary of risky business."

In the article about Slow Money on the CBC's website it's mentioned that one of the only growth industries in North America seems to be farmer's markets. The CBC's website goes on to add that "Slow Money takes its name from a culinary movement called Slow Food. For 20 years now, Slow Food proponents have advocated a lifestyle in which people take time to savour food and take pleasure in eating locally sourced products, rejecting large-scale farming and the hectic way of eating and living that damages our bodies and the world....

There is an exploding demand for what small farms and food producers have to offer. Yet banks see agriculture as a risky business, and brokers trade stock in agribusiness giants, not small, local operations. Farmers need cash and a system to get it to them. That's what Slow Money activists want to create: an investment system in which profit expectations are redefined so that big money can help small agricultural producers provide people with local, wholesome food." (Gutnik, David. "Putting your investments where your dinner is." CBC News. Web, 25 February 2009 <http://www.cbc.ca/news/world/story/2009/09/24/f-gutnick-slow-money.html>.)

So who's investing in the Slow Money movement? Woody Tasch is investing in organic Canadian farms.

The CBC article continues, "Until a few years ago, Tasch chaired an organization that connects investors with small businesses addressing social and environmental concerns. He was the matchmaker, funneling more than $130 million to hundreds of new ventures.

Businesses grew; foundations fulfilled their missions to do good works and investors made profits that were close to the stock market average. Everybody was happy.

But Tasch was hungry for a more focused approach that connected health, food and capital.

People investing in big, fast-operating companies expect big and fast returns. Tasch says that the Slow Money concept he came up with promotes the idea of nurturing capital—money that supports healthy enterprise with a modest return on investment." (Gutnik, David. "Putting your investments where your dinner is." CBC News. Web, 25 February 2009 <http://www.cbc.ca/news/world/story/2009/09/24/f-gutnick-slow-money.html>.)

Other investors include former high finance people like Cathy Berry. She made boatloads of money in the markets during the high tech boom in the '90s as a stock broker. She too now has been introduced to the concept of Slow Money...and quickly developed a love affair for the kind of outcomes it's helping to create.

"Berry hasn't seen much of a return on her investment yet. This is, after all, *slow* money. But she has deep pockets and is confident her optimism will pay off. In the meantime, she's trying to bring other investors on board. It hasn't been easy. 'I think we have got too hung up on "It's not a good investment unless we get a 20% return,"' she says. 'Why not think about loaning money for five per cent to your local farmer?'

Small is beautiful in the world of Slow Money—but so is big. There are more than 50,000 philanthropic foundations in the United States. Their assets total $400 billion US, most of it invested in the stock market. Needless to say, that money would be a game changer if it—or even a fraction of it—was reinvested in local agriculture." (Gutnik, David. "Putting your investments where your dinner is." CBC News. Web, 25 February 2009 <http://www.cbc.ca/news/world/story/2009/09/24/f-gutnick-slow-money.html>.)

The other key initiative that has communities coming together in a much different way is a concept known as "Transition Towns". "The main aim of the project generally, and echoed by the Towns locally, is to raise awareness of sustainable living and build local resilience in the near future. Communities are encouraged to seek out methods for reducing energy usage as well as increasing their own self-reliance—a slogan of the movement is 'Food feet, not food miles!' Initiatives so far have included creating community gardens to grow food; business waste exchange, which seeks to match the waste of one industry with another industry that uses this waste; and even simply repairing old items rather than throwing them away." ("Just What is a Transition Town, Anyway?" Transition Guelph. Web, January 2010 <http://transitionguelph.org/whatis.php>.)

It's a concept that's happening in North America too. Where I live in Toronto we have an organization with similar objectives. It's called Transition Toronto and was launched in 2009. The goal of the group in Toronto is to help the community manage more effectively if peak oil and climate changes occurred and made our normal way of life unmanageable. Transition Town Toronto helps communities come together with a new model of sustainability.

Where did this concept begin? What's its goal? If you do a little Google checking you will find that the concept started in the U.K.

"The Transition concept emerged from work permaculture designer Rob Hopkins had done with the students of Kinsale Further Education College in writing an 'Energy Descent Action Plan'. This looked at across-the-board creative adaptations in the realms of energy production, health, education, economy and agriculture as a "road map" to a sustainable future for the town. One of his students, Louise Rooney, set about developing the Transition Towns concept and presented it to Kinsale Town Council resulting in the historic decision by Councilors to adopt the plan and work towards energy independence.

So as you can see this "Transition Town" concept is here to stay…and it is a growing force.

Some examples of Transition Towns include: Totnes, England and Santa Cruz, New Mexico—two sites where transition towns have taken shape. There are also initiatives in Canada, the U.S., England, Australia, New Zealand and Italy." ("What are Transition Towns?" Oneness Publishing. Web, January 2010 <http://onenesspublishing.com/2011/12/transition-towns-2/>.)

If you want to learn more about either of these two socially minded initiatives log onto: http://transitionus.org/ and http://blog.lunapads.com/2009/11/green-investing-for-change/.

There is also one last way that we have to transform our communities first and that's with a local business lending organization called ACCESS Community Capital Fund. Its mandate is to help entrepreneurs get a head start.

"Let's face it, with job loss and our collective credit in some disarray, Access tends to turn the other cheek should you have financial challenges. What they are looking for is a great idea, mixed with character of the person and a plan to repay the loan. It's a starting loan...it's not big money...the maximum you can borrow is $5000.00. But if you're out of options and you've got that dream to start a business then Access might be up your alley.

The ACCESS Community Capital Fund, a Canadian Registered Charity, is a Community Loan Fund that helps small and emerging businesses in Toronto (Ontario, Canada) to meet their need for credit by securing initial loans of up to $5000. By granting small loans to local entrepreneurs, the ACCESS Community Capital Fund is contributing to the community as a whole—helping more people to become self-sufficient through self-employment." ("Social Enterprise." Community Foundations of Canada. Web, 9 January 2012 <http://cfc-cc.ca/programs/ri_funds_direct.html>.)

"ACCESS Community Capital Fund was formed to help promising entrepreneurs with viable business plans gain access to financing not available through other sources. Individual loans are made using a character based lending decision, where the abilities, skills and commitment of the applicant in conjunction with the strength of the business plan are key decision criteria." ("Matching Good Ideas With Capital." Access Community Capital Fund. Web, 9 January 2012 <http://www.accessccf.com/about_us>.)

Using a "step-lending" approach, ACCESS provides a series of loans that increase in size as the business grows in the community. You can obtain more information on Access online at: http://accessccf.com/.

Access is underfunded by Alterna Credit Union. Alterna is a local Credit Union with branches from Toronto east to Ottawa. They are one of very financial institutions that offer Micro

Business Loans to business clients. Micro Lending is a worldwide phenomenon made famous by Nobel Award winner Dr. Muhammad Yunus of the Grameen Bank. Dr. Yunus started a project that would lend money to the poor to help them start a business. It worked! It gave the local community, especially the women of the family hope and a chance to escape poverty, and thus the Micro Loan concept was born. Locally to where I live Alterna Savings offers the Micro Loans to those that cannot get money anywhere else. I have seen firsthand how the money Alterna lends has changed lives and helped the local small business economy grow.

Alterna acts as the finance company that backs up the Access Community loan fund.

Other sources of money include crowd funding. This is where you go online to the online community and source public funding for projects that you're launching. Do your homework on crowd funding and micro loans, because it may be just the start your business needs!

So as this year draws to a close and a new one begins...maybe it's about community. Maybe too we can forget about our problems a little if we help someone else out who needs it more. I recall the song the "Age of Aquarius" by the Fifth Dimension—we are entering the Aquarian Age now in fact and the line in the song went like this: "sympathy and understanding, truth and compassion abound".

I would like to think that through the hardships we've collectively gone through since 2009, that new ideas to make humanity fair for all will be the hope for us all in the future. To make a world that works for every woman, child and man. That's what I am playing for in the future...anyone want to join in?

AFTERWORD

So there you have it. My first book is in the books!

I hope it leaves you inspired. I hope you've learned a few things along our journey. Thanks for buying it and for being courageous to take the leap into starting or building your own business.

It's an exciting time to be alive. We are faced with so many challenges...so many opportunities...so much healing and so much work to be done in order to make the planet a better place to be. That's my goal for small business owners everywhere. We have a chance to do things right, to be ethical, to help others, to help heal the social and economic well being of our communities, to be people of peace who share, invest in and inspire ourselves and others.

Here now is an extra bonus...small business tips to help you be inspired each day. Enjoy!

These tips are from posts I have made on my Facebook profile...I put them up online about twice a week. Enjoy them...refer to them. They will help you with marketing, selling, managing money and just managing, period.

SMALL BUSINESS TIPS FOR SUCCESS

What could be better than a whole year's worth of tips? Here are 111 ways for you to be more successful from January through to December, every year...

JANUARY

Tip #1: How many of you have a business plan? If you don't have one then it's time to put one together. If you do have one then this is good time of year to dust it off...and see where you're at and where you want to go. Plus...don't forget to look at the numbers, no matter how bad or good they might be. Business planning is essential for you too. Here, size doesn't matter, but a good business plan does.

Tip #2: When creating or reviewing your plan, really assess the market. What is your ideal market? Who do you serve best? Who do you like to do business with? Personally, I work better with women than men, so I have to really look at that as a key market segment and get to understand that market more. This year take a half day a week to plan. You'll see a huge difference.

Tip #3: Last time out I mentioned taking a half day a week to research your market. Ask yourself this, when was the last time you made your way to a library to do some research, or to a Chamber of Commerce office, or a business resource centre in your area? These venues are chock full of information that can help you in your business. You can also check out the local economic development offices too. These are great places to get information, learn, get to know your market and ultimately succeed.

Tip #4: When you research you become an expert in your field. When you position yourself as a knowledgeable resource for your clients it sets you miles apart from your competitors. Just by researching, studying the marketplace, knowing your industry and of course being able to explain the benefits that your clients get from working with you, you will be able to position your business and stand out from the others.

Tip #5: Breathe, turn off the news and get away from the negativity. We're always being bombarded by negative news. As a small business owner it's tough not to let the news of the day get to you. So turn it off. Feed your mind with positive ideas and content; it helps a ton.

Tip #6: Follow your heart in business. For you analytical types that's almost heresy, but in this crazy mile-a-minute world, what choice do you have? Connect to your heart and let it soar as high as it can. We see examples every day of people giving from their heart when tragedy strikes. In a sea of crisis, people from all walks of life, of all personalities pitch in and help out. There is a coming together...no matter who you are...this coming together is about community. This notion of community helps us to keep our humanity. It keeps our hearts and the heart of our communities "beating" along!

Tip #7: One way to succeed in this marketplace is to team up. Tap into the power of joint ventures. When you team up you almost literally double the number of potential clients you can talk to instantly—providing of course the business owner you joint venture with has a solid contact list. Remember that a good joint venture can bring you more business and cut back on costs.

Tip #8: Talking about teaming up...who is on your team? Do you have a business mentor or a coach? Do you have a mastermind team? If you answered no to all of these then you might want to put these three items on your to-do list. I believe that if you think you can run your business alone you're in for a real eye opener. It's good to have a supporting cast—just ask an actor!

Tip #9: Get thee to the gym. One of my good colleagues in radio once told me that his most important appointment of the day wasn't with his best client but with himself at the gym. A good workout gives you peace of mind and balance, so that you can take on the fiercest competitor and tackle the biggest challenges with vim and vigour!

Tip #10: It's a hectic world and we talk about taking care of ourselves and *sharpening the saw* (as Dr. Stephen Covey suggests) because it's important to have balance in our businesses and work lives. Taking time out for prayer, meditation and visualization seemingly makes working easier to cope with. Create something big this year, but remember to take time for yourself.

Tip #11: One way to keep focused is through meditation and visualization. A few years back, I wanted to teach and get into a new line of work. I would visualize myself teaching every night before going to bed. Within one year I was teaching. When I pictured myself teaching it was in a room with pink walls; the room I actually taught in had pink walls. Go figure; it works!

Tip #12: Visualization, timeouts or a walk in the park...I had a sales manager that told me, "David sometimes you've got to take a walk in the park." He was in his 50s and I was in my late 20s then and I probably thought it was something old people needed to do, but now looking back, it makes sense. What's your walk in the park? Is it the gym, meditation, listening to good music? Just get into your own zone, so you can be more effective when your clients “come calling”.

Tip #13: We've been looking at balance in business. How much of the work you do really matters? By that I mean is the time you spend working getting you results? Making you money? If it isn't then you may want to delegate it to someone else. This week track your time to see where and how much you're wasting.

Tip #14: While we're still cautious about the economy…there are five reasons to be optimistic: 1) We’re all in this together. If so many countries and communities are being affected then change will happen. Be open to positive change, be a voice for positive economic change and take a stand for fairness and a new economy that works for everyone; 2) We haven’t even tapped into the green economy yet—I believe there is so much potential in that. We have a huge mess to clean up on this planet, one that will take years and millions of people to clean up; 3) The key to growth is really encouraging each individual on the planet to be a small business owner. If everyone has a gift, if everyone loves to do or make something…then imagine we’d literally have full employment or self-employment; 4) To me as long as we have problems in our lives we will need people to help solve and tend to those problems; and, 5) We need new ways of developing green, safe energy instead of relying on fossil fuels and hydroelectric and nuclear power that’s damaging to our health and environments. There is so much left to do, let's not lose hope...

Tip #15: Wow, the work week is so busy. Take time out to do something nice for someone else this weekend and spend time with people that matter. All work and no play...makes one kind of dull. So connect with family, play with your kids, go to a matinee, or meet up for a coffee with your friends or family and your clients. It's fun to be nice and it's nice to have fun!

Tip#16: What do you do with your time? How many of you have read a business book this month? Why not? If you need help in an area of your business, read a book...people with more experience than you have lived to tell the tale. Why not immerse yourself in a good book to help you improve your business skills and turn off American Idol, just for one night. Try it!

FEBRUARY

Tip #17: Who's your mentor? Seriously, how many of you have a mentor or a buddy that keeps you accountable? I mean, you could ask your spouse or significant other but do they really know the sweat and the passion you put into your business? A mentor or a buddy gives you the unbiased advice to help you in your business. Let's be honest, who can't use a little help along the way?

Tip #18: Want to know one of the best marketing tools I have used? It's got me jobs. It's got me rehired. It's built relationships. It's made my clients call me to thank me. It's made my clients laugh; it's made them feel all warm and fuzzy inside and it gets results. What is this wondrous thing?—a thank you note. Not enough of us use thank you notes. They work; send them and see for yourself!

Tip #19: Although a smile, a bottle of booze and a stuffed teddy bear do go a long way to thank your clients, sending simple hand written thank you notes can do more to *retain, obtain* and *reactivate* clients. In my business, I send thank you cards out all the time. It's not unusual to visit a client and see my card on their desk. Now that's a good feeling.

Tip #20: That personal touch...isn't that what we want when we do business with someone? How many of you have a contact management system where you can track conversations with clients, remember what they ordered last time and know their particular buying habits? If you can't afford the software make sure you use a filing system or track using Excel or Word. Just track the conversations you have with your clients and get to know them personally.

See my card still on their desks. The power of a thank you note...it's little, but it does a lot

Tip #21: Family Day is a holiday that has been established in several Canadian provinces. It brings to mind these questions: Where do you want to be investing your time? What really matters? Is it in family? Hanging out with friends? Painting a room in the house? Taking yoga? As Michael Gerber author of *The E-Myth* states, you start a business...not a death sentence. Take time to have balance; you'll feel better for it.

Tip #22: What do you do when it's slow? Panic? Worry? Cry? All good answers and believe me I have come close (if not actually done) all of these at some point in my business career. But none of these reactions helped. What did help was getting into action—cold calling, networking, planning, goal setting, going to trade shows...heck, even walking through a shopping mall to get ideas and get the juices flowing helps you. The key is to take action, any positive action, and to get moving!

Tip #23: Do you have an *Olympic* moment? In your business when did you strike gold? When business is slow or you're in a funk think back to the time you got your gold medal and tap into that energy, excitement and enthusiasm. Get back to the habits and thinking that got you the gold medal in your business and put those habits and mindset into play. Soon enough you'll be wearing a medal.

Tip #24: Melissa Hollingsworth of Canada's women's skeleton team came in 5th place. In her teary-eyed interview during her press conference she said she dared to dream big but came up short although not for lack of effort. This week, in your venture, life or work, dream big, but lose the attachment to winning—just enjoy the trip...

Tip #25: You know what the difference is between those that do well in their business as compared to those that struggle? It's about being hungry! Motivational speaker Les Brown talks about it in his seminars. "You've got to be hungry." What does being hungry mean? It means doing the things that no one else will and going beyond the call of duty.

Tip #26: When you watch a winning hockey team play you know that they won as a team. Who's on your team? Do you have a coach? A mentor? A mastermind team? My former mastermind group was about accountability and moving forward despite life's obstacles and challenges. Even just having a team around us makes us step up our game!

Tip #27: 1.6 seconds—that's the difference between a 5th place finish and a gold medal win. Not sure if you remember every athlete that competed in the Vancouver Winter Olympics a few years ago, but as a Canadian we of course got the "Canadian" perspective of the Olympics...and one person that stood out for me was a cross country skier, named Devon Kershaw. If you ask Devon what that amount of time meant to him he would tell you what it was like being so close to finishing first. Those few seconds put him in a 5th place finish after a grueling two hour race. A matter of seconds is the difference between a gold medal and a 5th place finish. It's that close sometimes. Life is like that too...and as I watched him race, I noticed that Devon skied his butt off too. But what do you do when you come in 2nd? You are still a winner. If you do your best...then you can never go wrong. For more on Devon, log onto http://www.devonkershaw.com/.

Tip #28: We've been talking about having a team; now it's time to talk about having creativity. "But wait," you say, "I am not creative!" That's not true—we're all creative. Coming up with an idea, looking at problem solving, figuring out ways to motivate your kids to get up and off to school each day is creative. But one thing you can do to get creative is to do something differently than you normally do. Take a different route to work and notice what you see.

Tip #29: We're taking on creativity. Play this game with me to see how creativity works. What's half of 13?

Most people answer six and a half. But in truth there are many more answers. Let your creativity run wild and see how many answers we can get. Think outside the box too for answers...this is the week to let your mind run wild...

Tip #30: Creativity—One way to tap into your creative process is to look at challenges and problems in a more proactive way. Or be open to a multitude of answers and be willing to look beyond the obvious. Perhaps just stop...take a timeout, step away, rejuvenate, go for that walk in the park and come at the problem refreshed. The alternative is to be stressed, bottled up and no good to anyone. I like to play a game with those I teach called "What's half of 13". If you put your mind to it there are dozens of answers all of which are correct. So what's half of 13? Any guesses? Can you come up with 10 of them?

Tip #31: So, the question was...what's half of 13? A few of you responded thinking outside the box, tapping into your creativity. Half of 13 is 13/2, 6.5, *thir* and *teen*, 10 and 3, X and III, half a baker's dozen, 7 and 6...there are more answers. When you put your mind to it creativity is easy to access...when we allow ourselves to step outside the lines. I think you get the point; when you're focused on a problem you can let your creativity take you to a new possibility!

Tip #32: Tap into your networks. I took a workshop on *social capital* today...What does *social capital* mean? It means leveraging your social networks with a goal to improve your economic or business status. It could mean getting a job or a new client. The trick is to access those that don't know you so you get warm welcome introductions to the contacts you need to make.

Tip #33: We're talking about marketing strategies. One notion I like is that *everything is marketing*—from how you dress, to how you answer the phone, to what your voice mail message says. Change your voice mail every day letting clients know when you'll call back. A generic voice mail doesn't outline where you are and at 4 p.m. when your client's getting nervous, a proper voicemail message will help ease your client's mind. It will stop clients from having to guess and wonder when you're going to call back.

Tip #34: Last time I said that marketing is in everything you do. Basically it's the law of attraction. The key though isn't to hope and pray for good things to happen...it's to *be* in action. Notice I said BE. Be the success you want to portray to your clients...be the leader, be the best, do the actions you need to do in order to be success filled!

Tip #35: The Law of Attraction...in marketing it means making yourself and business attractive to the client for them to want to work with you. How do you get a client to want to work with you and actually say, "Now this is a business I want to work with"? I believe it starts with professionalism, integrity and truth.

MARCH

Tip #36: We've been talking about the law of attraction and marketing all in one fell swoop. The LOA is about making you stand out from the crowd. So this week pick one area of your business that you can stand out in and make it even better. The road to success begins with one step at a time...so what's outstanding about your business venture? Do you have an operations manual? Can you work on one area of your business that needs working on and master it? Once you've mastered one area of your venture then work on the next. Be your best this month!

Tip #37: What is that one area of your business that you can shine in? Is it in your customer service promise? What's going to WOW the customer? Marketing expert Tad Hargrave introduced me to Dr. Paddi Lund. He's a dentist that was almost suicidal until he flipped his business model to be about creating an experience for the client that was so exquisite he broke the mold as to how a dental practice should be run. What are you going to do that's just "exquisite"?

Tip #38: We've been talking about the nice warm and fluffy stuff...but don't lose sight that you're in business. That means you have to focus on the business...get the money equation discussed, set the expectations, ask your client what they expect and want, deliver on your promises, get sign offs on important documents, etc. Address anything that might ruin the relationships you work so hard to develop!

Tip #39: No one likes processes...but they are necessary for you to do what you do. A process is like a recipe, describing how you do what you do. Try taking on a section of your business each month and develop the recipe for how you conduct business. Make it so what you do is easy to do. When it's easy to follow your employees can catch on fast allowing you a little more time off work for good behaviour!

Tip #40: Part of your process must focus on consistency. Your clients don't want to be guessing about who you are and what you are about. They don't like change. So be consistent in all areas of your business. Like them or not but McDonald's is consistent. Starbucks is very consistent. What about Heinz Ketchup? You've got to be consistent; don't leave your clients guessing as to who or what your business is about!

Tip #41: Do you know what your best client's favourite charities are? Back in the day, my best clients supported the Kids Help Phone Foundation. I joined in and volunteered my time for five years. I got more out of it then I put in, but I got closer to my best clients and they got to see me in a much different light. What light do you want to be seen in?

Tip #42: There are a few books about bringing "soul" back into an organization. For example there is *Chicken Soup for the Soul at Work*, *The Corporate Mystic* and *Reclaiming Higher Ground.* What does your business do to make a "soul" connection? By this I mean do you inspire people—your employees and your clients?

Tip #43: Watch your thinking. If your thoughts are about not being enough...not good enough, not smart enough, not rich enough, not pretty or handsome enough, who are those thoughts really serving? Are they helping you? Or are they keeping you small? Thank the thought, change the thought, affirm a new positive thought and commit to take proactive steps forward. That way you can serve humanity!

Tip #44: So if you're thinking negatively about yourself, how will your customers perceive you? The bottom line is you've got to love yourself as is.

Yes...you may not be fully baked...but you can commit to being the best you there is. If you can't break free from the past and the limits you have put on yourself then begin to parent the inner child inside...and watch that inner child bust loose...it's magic!

Tip #45: We're talking about working with your inner child. During a past job loss I worked with mine. Filled with fear and about to be fired by my manager (like a kid being punished) as the adult I had to assure him all was fine. When meeting with my manager I told her that my inner child was really hurt. Yes, I lost the gig but she retained me to coach 10 clients, keeping me active while I regrouped. No fear for this kid!

Tip #46: Don't think for a moment that you can ignore the inner game. People buy people they like. Being liked drives sales. What are you doing to be likable? Usually it's the little things, like a thank you note or a "hi, how are you" call...just because. If you're happy inside, then your clients will notice that in you. This week be likable—like yourself first because you matter to a lot of people and you know what? I like you a lot!

APRIL

Tip #47: You're wondering what you have to do to be liked around here. It's usually the little things like responding to people in a timely fashion, staying in touch, sending thank you notes, going for a coffee with a client just because, listening, doing what you say, saying what you do, being your word, being respectful and showing that you care. These things all add up. They're small but huge. Be huge this week!

Tip #48: Earth Day Biz Tip. As business owners we're not entirely clear as to what it means to be a green business. There is no clear cut green plan for us to follow. Common sense is your best ally. Do things in your business that cut back on waste and energy consumption and recycle. If you want to learn more about going *green* tap into a local "Green Business Initiative" in your area. One such organization is Green Drinks. Google that and chances are you will find a business meeting in your area. It's a chance for "Green" businesses to gather and network.

Tip #49: I advised you earlier to take a different route to work. What did you notice that you don't normally notice? In life and in business we need to notice the small things. They make a difference. Yes, we can bemoan our fate, and yes maybe right now things look bleak, but if you look deeper at the route you're on you'll realize that you've got lots to be thankful for. Now go get 'em!

Tip #50: A few years ago, I reached a personal milestone: I had written my 50th tip and reached 600 friends on Facebook too. At that time I was really happy to have reached these targets. I have doubled my friends list and am in my third series of business tips on Facebook...but you know it's nice to celebrate reaching the milestones in your life and business. You need to recognize the little events that occur and just give yourself a pat on the back. Little successes lead to the big ones. So celebrate this week!

Tip #51: Remember the recession in '90-'91. The news was so bad you didn't want to get up out of bed. This time around...change that pattern. Just go for it! Get jump started. Get on that project you've put off, meet that client at 8 a.m. for tea, workout early, and get a kick start on your day. Be a poster child for taking action. Why? Who would you want to do business with? Exactly! Y-O-U, because *you* are in action!

MAY

Tip #52: You have to be okay with the unexpected. You can't take the seemingly bad things that happen personally, or as my British mom would say, "Chin up, let's go...come on, hip, hip." You see in this day and age, the world is calling you. There are people who need help; there is room for terrific new ideas; there's a mess to clean up (environmentally) and lots of work to do to mend the planet. What are you mending?

Tip #53: Recognize your mom on Mother's Day. Chances are you went to the "Bank of Mom and Dad" for financing in the early days or you got some good advice from your mom about your venture. In fact you tap into your feminine side for intuition, creativity and nurturing so be thankful for what your mom passed on to you genetically and always run your business in a way that would make your momma proud!

Tip #54: The key to good marketing is your ability to communicate your value. What is value? Value is the sum of the benefits that you offer your clients minus the cost. The key benefits are: product benefits, service benefits, relationship benefits and brand benefits. For your product and service benefits you need to get clear on what makes you so good. Tell people what makes you so special and don't hold back!

Tip #55: We are talking benefits and value. You have to let your clients know what they get from you. What do you do to help them get the results they want? A product benefit example is spinach...it's chock full of nutrients, helps prevent cancer and is well-priced. An example of a service benefit is FedEx, when it has to get there next day or else. What do you excel at that it is the core of your marketing message?

Tip #56: Why is it that I have been talking about value and benefits as two key ingredients in your marketing message? It's because they are what your clients want to hear in order for them to stop and take note of you. It's like music to their ears, the cha ching in their pocket, the cherry on top of a...float. Value and benefits answer the "What's in it for me?" question that your clients are asking.

Tip #57: Don't minimize your value. Learn from your existing clients why they buy from you and what made them choose you to work with. There is gold in knowing. Your clients will let you know that it's about service, or integrity, or that you are consistent. Whatever those reasons are, work them into your marketing messaging...because that's what makes you good at what you do.

Tip #58: It's tough to get back into things after a long weekend—if only we had more time to chill by the lake, or have another cold one with friends, or enjoy that steak on the BBQ just once more. You know after having a wonderful long weekend that you need to make sure you plan for a little "fun" or "you time" more often; it does the soul and your bottom line good.

JUNE

Tip #59: What happens if you have no idea what to do next? You improvise! When writing these tips...especially today, I had no idea what I was going to talk about...so I looked at that challenge and thought I'd discuss it with you . My rich uncle once said, “Fake it 'til you make it.” Today be okay with being in the zone of the unknown, improvise and play! It will re-energize you!

Tip #60: In these challenging times, what do you do to make sense of it all? It's about finding your centre. *Getting back to basics* means leading a balanced life. You want to make sure that you have a healthy mix of work/business goals along with your health, spiritual, social, family goals as well. Each day make sure you spend time on each part of your life...and I promise you you'll be in the zone.

Tip #61: I used to have a boss that told me to have a walk in the park sometimes. At 27 I didn't relate to that at all but now at my age I get it. Sometimes in order to be fresh, in order to be vital, in order to be effective you have to step away from the business of running your business...besides who's in charge here? This week, walk in the park and see how much more effective you are.

Tip #62: I have been hearing that business is slow for a lot of people. People aren't spending, it's quiet, we're worried...and yes it's true...but remember this...each day around the world there are trillions of dollars being spent. You've just got to get a small little piece of that money. It’s out there...get into action, make an extra five calls to prospects and go get it!

Tip #63: This week, watch what you're giving energy to. Is it anything that you can control? Is it a complaint about someone or a situation? Can you control it? Can you change it? If not move on and begin to create a new game for yourself. Choose to do something you can change. Invest your time, energy and money into a cause that lights you up and turns you on. Have a sexy week!

Tip #64: About a month ago, I spoke at a Chamber of Commerce (not naming names) and asked the audience if they had a business plan. Less than half had one. You need a few things to be successful in business. First is vision, second passion and drive, third is a good business plan, fourth flexibility, and fifth, a willingness to shift gears if things are just not working out and you're getting "push back". And the last thing you need that might help your business is a rich uncle. I mean it couldn't hurt right? Now go make it happen!

Tip #65: Last time I talked about the things you need to be a good business owner. My comment about having a rich uncle got a lot of reaction. But seriously, where do you go for money if your business needs it? The number one place is yourself, then friends and family, then your suppliers, the fourth place are banks/credit unions and finally, check out government grants/programs by logging onto http://www.ontario.ca/en/business_program/categories/ont04_036384.

Just a word of caution, no matter where you live, check with your local government resources or Chamber of Commerce first before checking into possible grants. In this economy, grants are not as available and they are very sector specific. There are some "for profit" companies who are capitalizing on selling you the false hope of access to grants, when really they're just selling their guide books. Do your homework, go to a government source or your local Chamber first; they should have information on available (legal) grants for your business and will help guide you to the organizations that have money to lend. I hope this info helps!

Tip #66: Money—I don't have any; I'm broke, and money doesn't grow on trees. These are money conversations going on in our heads. On the count of three...1, 2, 3...what else can you tell yourself about money? Try, "Money loves me and comes to me easily" or "I am a money magnet" or "I am worthy to accept abundance!" The truth is even the richest people never think they have enough...so why kvetch about it? Think positive!

Tip #67: Money is really just energy—it ebbs and it flows. You get paid, money comes in and then it goes back out. Yet, we give it so much attention. It consumes our thoughts, worries us and yes we have beliefs about it that don't make sense. This weekend think about your money story—like time, it's usually something we don't have enough of. Act like you have total abundance! See what you can enjoy without spending a lot!

Tip #68: Where would you be without your dad? To start you wouldn't be here. Seriously, your dad probably gave you guidance, money, maybe even a swift kick in the butt. My dad was a true gentleman. He was wise and funny. He died too soon for my liking, but he left me with this: As a kid I asked how much a clown made. He replied, "What do you care what a clown makes, do it and be happy!" Happy Fathers Day!

JULY

Tip #69: Never undersell yourself. Never cut prices or discount without being asked. Case-in-point, take Paul Henderson, the guy that scored that amazing winning goal in the '72 Canada Russian hockey summit. He auctioned off his hockey jersey. He didn't think he'd get a lot of money for it but he ended up getting one million dollars. Bottom line, value is in the eyes of your customer, not you! Go make some money!

Tip #70: Halfway through any year you need to ask yourself if you have achieved the goals that you planned at the start of the year. If not, why not? Check in and see if the goal has the same pull or importance now that it did then. If not, now is a good time to reassess where you're at and where you want to go. The key to meeting your goal is you've got to really want it badly. This week set a goal like your life depends on it!

Tip #71: I spent Canada Day with friends, at the gym, working and then at a Canada Day event (concert and fireworks). It made me think about how grateful I am to live in Canada. Yes, it's not perfect, but it's still an amazing country—a country we can shape and where we're still free to live our dreams and passions. This weekend be grateful for what you have. It feels good.

Tip #72: Summer is here for sure...it's hot, steamy, and it's time to go easy and take it slow. Slow is good sometimes. It gives you a chance to catch your breath, catch up on paperwork, connect with clients over a BBQ, plan for the future, revise your business plans, revisit your marketing approach and nurture business relationships that need tending too. So enjoy the lazy, hazy, crazy days of summer!

Tip #73: I met a great woman at a business event I was at recently. Meet Bette Jean Crews, president of the Ontario Farming Association—she was a panelist at a Green Business Forum. She drove from Trenton to be in Guelph, Ontario for the event—that's about a three hour drive and to top it off she just came back from shooting the rapids in the Fraser River in British Columbia (the western edge of Canada)...which made her journey even longer. Bette is 63 with four kids. I was curious as to what she learned about herself on this trip. "I am not my age," she replied. She certainly isn't, she loves life and lives it full on! What beliefs do you need to bust up about yourself, your age or your current circumstances to get to your goal and live life fully like Bette?

Tip #74: Be in the moment. A lot can happen when you're just living in the moment. You're focused, you're creative and you're able to block out distractions, past memories and future worries. Some call it mindfulness; some call it being in the zone. Today, practice being in the moment, right here, right now and see how it helps you in your business and in life.

Tip #75: Last week, I talked about being in the moment and wouldn't you know it...the British Open winner Louis Oosthuizen said that that was the place he was in and that focus helped win the tourney. Mind over matter—train your mind not to wander off into negative thoughts or negative outcomes but to think positive thoughts and positive outcomes. This week pay attention to your inner dialogue.

Tip #76: Here's a challenge! What's one area of your life or business you really want to change? It could be an improvement in organizing your space, or taking off 10 pounds, or hiring someone to sell for you. Over the next 30 days, draw up a plan and be relentless about achieving this goal...where you'll stop at nothing and do whatever it takes. Be the author of your life!

Tip #77: Just for today, give of yourself freely, without any expectation of getting something back in return. Give advice or help a customer with a problem. Just give it away...and like a boomerang watch what comes back to you. It's not in us normally to give something away without an expectation for something in return. Today lose the expectation and allow for whatever it is to come to you!

Tip #78: Alan, Lydia and Muhammad are my *former* co-workers where I worked. Six weeks ago they were told their contracts weren't going to be renewed. Friday was their last day at work. These are people who never once quit. They worked hard and were part of the team to the end. They had plenty of reasons to slack off and feel sorry for themselves, but they didn't. They were true professionals all the way! This week, be a professional in all you do!

AUGUST

Tip #79: I don't talk much about being organized but clutter limits your effectiveness. Some say your car is your life...so if it's a messy car...it's a messy life. As we move through August take time to declutter...and clean up messes. Messes can be physical messes or messes with friends or family and in business relationships. When you clean up, you clean up your life too. Now where is that Endust?

Tip #80: Here are three ways to save money and time: 1. Hire a student to help you in your business; school starts soon and students can do their co-op in a variety of ways to help you. 2. Check where you may be overspending in your business; do a thorough check to see where you can cut costs. 3. Really shop for deals, use coupons, look at bankruptcy deals, close outs and motivated sellers.

Tip #81: When was the last time you shut it all down? No work, no phone, no cell, no Internet? Try it for a day this weekend...shut it down and connect to your “inner” self. You see the inner game helps your outer game...but we focus on the outer way too much. This weekend go for a yoga class, a walk along the lake or take a book to the beach...your inner and outer game will thank you. Go team!

Tip #82: It's a full moon tonight. When was the last time you grew hair on your chest and howled at the moon? Sometimes, we need to do that. Ok, maybe we don’t need to grow hair on our chest but we all need a good howl to dump anger, pain or hurts every once in a while. I suggest a good scream alone in the car, writing a mean letter (you don’t need to actually send it), going to a forest and screaming at a tree and then hugging it...or punching a punching bag. Ok on the count of three, 1, 2, 3...HOWL!

Tip #83: Doggy, Doggy, Pogo Dogs, and Cotton Candy, getting sick as you come off the roller coaster or the Scrambler, loud music, hot sun, big crowds...it’s fabulous!!! It’s the Ex...or as it’s officially called “The CNE” (Toronto’s annual exhibition since 1879). The CNE brings good memories...What are you doing that's memorable? What can you do so that your clients will think fondly about you in years to come? Not that serving clients pogo dogs is part of the equation, but it’s important to do something that will have your customers thinking about you in years ahead. Now let's go hit some rides!

Tip #84: There is a great Hindu quote that says, "Have patience, in time even grass becomes milk." Everything changes in time. Don't be in a hurry to rush the process. Do your due diligence. Look after the details: take time to make sure you've taken care of all the details of each part of your business from how you answer the phones, to how you get a customer. Identify the details and work on perfecting them. You have to make friends with the little things that need to be done in order to accomplish your end goal. Be patient...your vision will come true if you chip away at it each day...I promise!

SEPTEMBER

Tip #85: This time of year is akin to a new year. Take time in the next week to think about what you want to accomplish for the balance of the year. Usually you create from your values. What is it that you value?—is it freedom, peace, abundance or creativity? Whatever you want to create this year, make sure it's in alignment with your values. Your values are the fuel to your fire.

Tip #86: Fall is in the air today. With that comes a bit of sadness, a summer that went far too fast yet again. What do you do when you feel flat? You can talk it out or journal. But be okay with the feeling and the emotions. What you want to do is to find hope in the change that occurs. Life does go on; it's got ups and downs and we've got to be able to move through them with ease and love wherever we're at.

Tip #87: The kids went back to school yesterday...ready and eager to learn. What about *your* education? Do you have a training budget? Is learning something you do regularly? Can you teach an old dog new tricks? You bet! Don't be so sure you know it all. Plan to seek out wise teachers through tele-classes, workshops, books and CDs. Watch how you improve almost any aspect of your business and all within budget!

Tip #88: Breathe in. Can you feel it? The fall air, a time to get going, organizing, getting into shape, or starting a new eating plan (diet is a four letter word). In your business, what are key areas you need to work on? Is it business development, processes, operations, sales? Focus on one area in your business and just seek to do all you can to improve between now and Christmas and watch what happens!

Tip #89: Don't quit...even if you're out of the running give it your best shot. I love baseball...especially the Blue Jays. It happens that sometimes they are out of the running for a playoff spot but they continue to play well as a team and they go out giving it their all each game. This week ask yourself if you are giving it your all each game. If not, why not, what's holding you back from being the star that you are?

Tip #90: What are you committed to change in your life or business? What's your legacy? My friend Vin organized a concert to protest diesel trains in the Eglinton/Weston Rd. area in Toronto. This is a residential area but it's a poorer part of town. What do the trains going through mean to local residents? The trains mean noise and pollution and Vin took a stand and did so in a proactive way. What are you doing in your business to take a stand and say "No, I won't settle for the way things are anymore"? This week be a rebel.

OCTOBER

Tip #91: When Cito Gaston retired as manager of the Toronto Blue Jays baseball team he received a standing ovation from the fans. Cito ran the team he lead with dignity, grace and he always played hard and wanted to win badly. I think in business that's how you've got to manage. Manage with dignity but be hungry to win and work both hard and smart. If you do...you might get a standing ovation from 33,000 fans too!

Tip #92: As you see the colour of the leaves change you might think about what leaves you need to change in your business or life? What aspect of your business needs some colour? Is it in your selling style or your overall look? Maybe, you need to add colour to your marketing or customer relations? Maybe you need to look at how you attract, keep and yes, even reactivate past clients. Make it a colour-filled week!

Tip #93: What if someone wrote you off and said that you didn't have much potential to make it? What would you do? Would you give up? Or stay the course, make adjustments, get coaching, and make the most of every opportunity that came your way? I hope you'd make the most of opportunities and not give up. Records get broken every day by people who won't give up.

Tip #94: Sometimes you've just got to get down...throw the phone away, turn off the computer and relax. Take a walk, see a movie, go dancing, do a yoga class...sometimes you need a mini-vacation from it all. Don't worry, the work will be there tomorrow...I assure you...but from 3 p.m. on..."get down"...get away from the crazy pace!

Tip #95: We waited in anticipation after the Chilean mining accident to see if there would be any survivors. Florencio Avalos will go down in history as the first Chilean miner to be rescued. What went through his mind through the ordeal? Was his faith tested? How did he manage to keep it together? And after the ordeal the survivors had to ride up to the surface in a tight capsule spinning its way up through the earth for 20 minutes. Next time you think you've got a challenge, remember Florencio and the other miners. That's a huge challenge.

Tip #96: So I mentioned that good news story about the Chilean miners that happened a few years ago. We held a local celebration when we heard the news. Big companies got on board as well. IKEA committed to installing solar energy panels to power up their business; Oakville said no to a gas power plant, opting for cleaner energy; and the Government of Canada suggested we need to do business outside of Canada in order to grow our businesses. This was some really good news all around. Let's focus on the positive in the news at all times and be solution providers in our businesses!

Tip #97: What do you really want? What is it in your life or business that would give you crazy amounts of passion, purpose, play and prosperity? These aren't the five Ps you learned in marketing class, but they are the four Ps that are key to success. We're at a junction in life where passion, purpose, play and prosperity are what it's really about. If we focus on those four things then watch how beautifully life will flow.

Tip #98: Well...Halloween is upon us and it makes me ask, "What's spooking you?" For some it's the economy, for others it's the disorganized mess in the office and for others it's a bad client. So here is the challenge and the tip. Ask five people for feedback about how to handle what's spooking you and then ask them to hold you accountable to taking action. Deal? Ghoul...er...I mean cool!

Tip #99: Fall time is so romantic. You can walk in the leaves, wear a big wool sweater and breathe in the cool crisp air. Awww...romance! But how are you romancing your customers? What would your best customer say about you if I asked him? This week think of three things you can do to romance your customer? Maybe take him to lunch, bring in a pizza or send him a note. Ooooh, I feel romantic and I am giggly!

Tip #100: Never thought I would reach 100 tips. Was going to stop at 52...one for each week of the year...but these tips keep coming to mind and I am glad to share. Today's tip is how Halloween and running a business are alike. You shouldn't be afraid to ask for the sale...just like asking for candy, asking for the sale is even sweeter...especially if the clients say yes.

Tip #101: So...why is being in business like Halloween?—word of mouth for one. If you can orchestrate enough good vibes for your business...the world will beat a path to your door. Just like the coolest house with the best treats in the neighbourhood, the word gets out and the kids come to your place for good candies and your customers will find you too!

NOVEMBER

Tip #102: I went into my local neighbourhood restaurant on Friday and according to them business is way down. They are blaming it on the economy and the fact that the mall they're in is going through some major changes...two of the biggest tenants had just moved out. Funny thing, I went to another restaurant in another part of town that sells the same food and they were packed. If you sense that business is down, reconnect with your clients, ask them what they want, innovate, change, and grow. Don't *let* it happen, *make* it happen!

Tip #103: Having a niche is nice. I was interviewed on a Punjabi radio show. I was promoting my work and the training programs we run at the Learning Enrichment Foundation. We help newcomers settle in, learn the basics and adapt to a new life in Canada. Tapping into niche markets is a great way to grow your business. After the interview I got two calls from excited/motivated listeners. Want success? Find your niche.

Tip #104: Sometimes you just don't feel like doing it...today is one of those days. So what do you do? The answer is that you take baby steps. Do one thing; start something. Just take a small step forward towards what it is you need to do. I recommend starting with the most fun things first. Leave the dirty work to another time, when you're more prepared to take that on. So go get 'em...just start.

Tip #105: Ooooh, it is getting cold; time to warm up. Here are two ways to warm up your sales: 1) Care for your clients...meet, plan, and really see how you can help them this year and into the next; and, 2) Do something good for the community...volunteer, deliver food hampers, work at an Out of the Cold program—just give back. When you do you are rewarded tenfold!

Tip #106: It's November—Grey Cup time! It's cold and perhaps not the greatest weather to be playing football in. But the players don't seem to care and why is that? They have a goal in mind. They want to win and they aren't going to let any obstacles get in their way—including the weather. Keep your focus and you can overcome the greatest obstacles and achieve what you believe. This week go for the long bomb and score yourself a touchdown!

DECEMBER

Tip #107: The holiday season has begun...it's a great time of year too. I love it because people are kind to each other. I like it for business because it's a great time to connect to your clients, book a lunch or that annual planning meeting and see how you can really help your clients next year. Help them reach their goals, be of total service to them and watch the results! Jingle all the way!

Tip #108: Remember watching a "Christmas Carol" during the holidays? Ebenezer Scrooge realized that his past was going to create a dismal future. The ghosts of the past came to haunt him and show him how to make the changes necessary to live a life of joy, abundance and gratitude. So today, what would you change in order to live a life like that—a life without regrets? "Bless us everyone!"

Tip #109: Typically December is the time of year to look inside, review and plan. It's the time we *wrap up* the year. It's also a time to connect with friends, family and those less fortunate than we are. Give back, help out at a food bank, or shelter...but as you do, assess and review how far you've come since the beginning of the year. It's a time to see where you want to go in the future. Think it through and then write it down. Here is a link to a mission statement builder: http://www.franklincovey.ca/FCCAWeb/aspx/library_mission.htm. I hope it helps.

Tip #110: Today is a good day to start something. Take your most pressing issue and just take that first step forward, make that first call or put a plan into action. Just take that first step. When you achieve a goal, you realize that you can achieve another and another. All of a sudden you build up your goal *setting* muscles and confidence and you become a rocking amazing goal *getter*. Today, be a goal getter!

Tip #111: When Mark Dailey, a respected broadcaster, friend and colleague, passed away it made the news. In everything I read not one person had a bad word to say. What a legacy to leave. He was kind, encouraging, open, and a friend to many in the broadcasting biz and outside too. What trail are you blazing? What's your legacy?

ABOUT THE AUTHOR

David Cohen has been in sales and marketing since 1986. In 1999 a career and life shift occurred and he began to coach and train small business owners and hasn't looked back. Since then, David has taught over 1500 clients through various government sponsored small business development training initiatives and programs. He's also spoken at conferences, trade shows and business networking groups. He's a dynamic speaker and coach that comes from the heart and soul.

Today, David is a business coach and facilitator working with new business start-ups in the Ontario Self Employment Benefit program in Whitby and he has headed up the Entrepreneurship Training Programs for Newcomers to Canada at the Learning Enrichment Foundation. He also does work with Future Watch a leading Environmental learning organization, Job Skills and the Youth Employment Services on two of their youth small business programs.

David is a sought after coach and speaker in both the nonprofit and for profit business organizations as well.

David was also the host and producer of the Small Business Big Ideas Radio Show from its start-up ten years ago (August 17th, 2002) on CKDO 1580 AM and 107.7 FM in Oshawa. He re-launched the radio show online on "Radio That Doesn't Suck" dot com in May 2011.

13010124R00152

Made in the USA
Charleston, SC
11 June 2012